Practice is the best way to prepare for the 9-1 GCSE Maths exams...

...and with two full sets of Higher Level Practice Papers, this CGP pack has everything you need to make sure you're 100% ready!

It's perfectly matched to the new Grade 9-1 requirements, so the papers are just like the ones you'll tackle in the real exams. They're a great way to find out how well you're progressing towards your target grade.

We've also included fully worked answers and mark schemes, making it easy to see where your strengths are — and which topics need a bit more practice.

The Three Big Ways to Improve Your Score

1) **Try all of these practice papers**
   These practice papers contain questions in the same style, at the same level and covering the same topics as the questions you could get in the real exam. The more practice you get, the less chance of a nasty surprise on your exam.

2) **Keep practising the things you get wrong**
   The whole point of a practice exam is to find out what you don't know*. So every time you get a question wrong, revise that subject then have another crack at it.

   *Use the mark scheme in this booklet to help you see where you dropped your marks.

3) **Don't throw away easy marks**
   Always answer the question the way it's asked — if it asks for units, use the right ones. Always double-check your answer and don't make silly mistakes — obvious really.

CGP

GCSE
Mathematics
For the Grade 9-1 Course

Practice Exam Papers
Instructions & Answer Book
Higher Tier

Exam Set MHB45 / MXHP43

© CGP 2016 — copying more than 5% of this booklet is not permitted

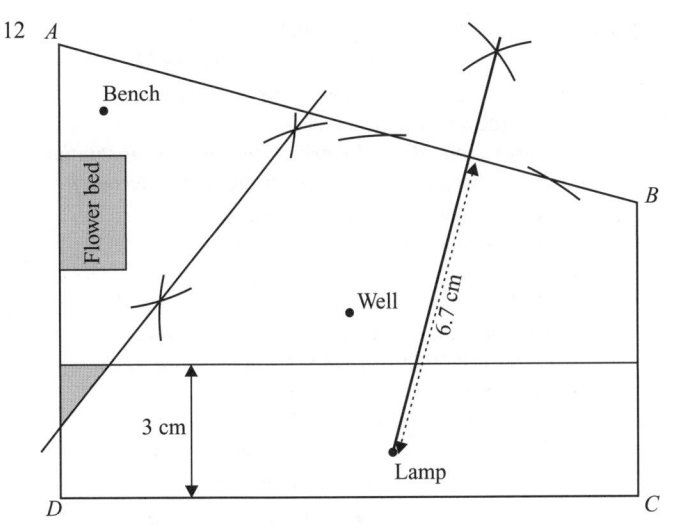

12 a) See diagram for construction lines.
   [3 marks available — 1 mark for correct construction lines, 1 mark for line equidistant to bench and well, 1 mark for correct shaded area]

   b) 6.7 cm = 6.7 m — see diagram for construction lines.
   [2 marks available — 1 mark for correct construction lines, 1 mark for correct answer]

13 a) For each class, multiply the class width by the frequency:

Time taken (t)	$0 < t \leq 10$	$10 < t \leq 15$	$15 < t \leq 20$	$20 < t \leq 30$	$30 < t \leq 60$
Frequency	25	48	36	28	15

[2 marks available — 2 marks for all correct frequencies, otherwise 1 mark for at least two correct frequencies]

   b) 8:40 am – 8:15 am = 25 minutes. To estimate the number of students who take 25 minutes or more, take half of those in the range $20 < t \leq 30$ plus all of those in the range $30 < t \leq 60$, which is $\frac{28}{2} + 15 = 29$ students. So 29 students need to leave before 8:15 to arrive at school on time.
   [3 marks available — 1 mark for identifying the correct time, 1 mark for identifying the correct values in the table to match the time, 1 mark for finding the correct answer]

14 Opposite angles in a cyclic quadrilateral add up to 180° so
   $5x + 12° + x + 18° = 180°$ *[1 mark]*, which gives $6x + 30° = 180°$, and so $6x = 150°$ and $x = 25°$. *[1 mark]*
   Angle $BCD = 5 \times 25° + 12° = 125° + 12° = 137°$.
   $137° + 43° = 180°$ so BCD and ADC are allied angles. *[1 mark]*
   BC is parallel to AD and $ABCD$ is a trapezium. *[1 mark]*
   [4 marks available in total — as above]

15 a) $u_1 = 5$
   $u_2 = 5^2 - (3 \times 5) - 1 = 9$ *[1 mark]*
   $u_3 = 9^2 - (3 \times 9) - 1 = 53$ *[1 mark]*
   [2 marks available in total — as above]

   b) $u_1 = 3$
   $u_2 = 3^2 - (3 \times 3) - 1 = -1$
   $u_3 = (-1)^2 - (3 \times -1) - 1 = 3$ *[1 mark]*
   This pattern repeats, so the even terms = –1 and the odd terms = 3, *[1 mark]* so $u_{171} = 3$ *[1 mark]*
   [3 marks available in total — as above]

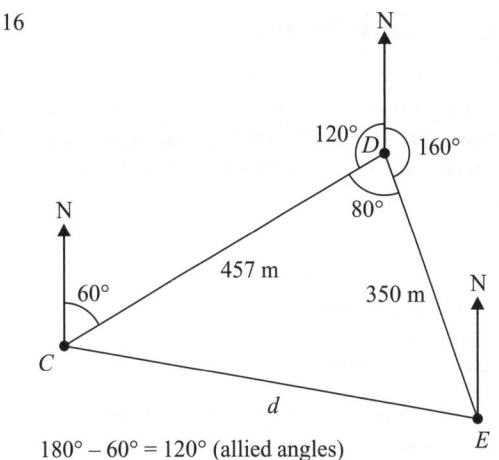

16 $180° - 60° = 120°$ (allied angles)
   Angle $CDE = 360° - 120° - 160° = 80°$ (see diagram).
   Let d be the direct distance from C to E. Using the cosine rule,
   $d^2 = 457^2 + 350^2 - 2 \times 457 \times 350 \times \cos 80° = 275\,798.948...$
   so $d = \sqrt{275\,798.948...} = 525.1656... $ m $= 525.2$ m (1 d.p.)
   [4 marks available — 1 mark for finding angle CDE, 1 mark for using the cosine rule with appropriate values, 1 mark for correctly calculating the value of d^2 using the cosine rule, 1 mark for the correct answer]

17 If r is the radius and h is the height of the small cone, then the full cone will have height $2h$ and radius $2r$. *[1 mark]*
   Volume of small cone = $\frac{1}{3}\pi r^2 h$
   Volume of full cone = $\frac{1}{3}\pi(2r)^2 \times 2h = \frac{8}{3}\pi r^2 h$ *[1 mark]*
   Volume of frustum = $\frac{8}{3}\pi r^2 h - \frac{1}{3}\pi r^2 h = \frac{7}{3}\pi r^2 h$ *[1 mark]*
   Ratio of small cone : frustum = $\frac{1}{3}\pi r^2 h : \frac{7}{3}\pi r^2 h = 1 : 7$ *[1 mark]*
   [4 marks available in total — as above]

18 Gradient of $OP = \frac{-6-0}{-8-0} = \frac{-6}{-8} = \frac{3}{4}$ *[1 mark]*
   Gradient of tangent is the negative reciprocal, which is $-\frac{4}{3}$. *[1 mark]*
   $y = mx + c$ where m is the gradient, and c is the y-intercept:
   so $y = -\frac{4}{3}x + c$ *[1 mark]*
   Substitute in point P to find c:
   $-6 = -\frac{4}{3}(-8) + c$
   $-6 = \frac{32}{3} + c$, so $c = -\frac{50}{3}$
   The equation of line l is $y = -\frac{4}{3}x - \frac{50}{3}$ *[1 mark]*
   [4 marks available in total — as above]

19 The perimeter = 1, so $2\left(\frac{1}{3x} + \frac{x}{6}\right) = 1$
   So, $2\left(\frac{1}{3x} + \frac{x}{6}\right)$ *[1 mark]*
   $= 2\left(\frac{3x^2 + 6}{18x}\right) = 6\left(\frac{x^2 + 2}{18x}\right) = \frac{x^2 + 2}{3x} = 1$ *[1 mark]*
   $x^2 + 2 = 3x$
   $x^2 - 3x + 2 = 0$
   $(x - 1)(x - 2) = 0$ *[1 mark]*
   So, $x = 1$ or $x = 2$ *[1 mark]*
   Substituting $x = 2$: $AB = \frac{1}{6}$, $BC = \frac{1}{3}$,
   but AB is supposed to be longer than BC, so $x \neq 2$
   Substituting $x = 1$: $AB = \frac{1}{3}$ miles and $BC = \frac{1}{6}$ miles *[1 mark]*
   [5 marks available in total — as above]

Set 2 Paper 3 — Calculator

1. a) $3x + 5y + 7y - 9x - y = -6x + 11y$ *[1 mark]*
   b) $20x^3y + 8xy^2 = 4xy(5x^2 + 2y)$
   [2 marks available — 1 mark for taking out one common factor correctly (4, x or y), 1 mark for the complete correct factorisation]
   c) $\dfrac{3x + 4}{2} = \dfrac{5x + 3}{3}$
   $3(3x + 4) = 2(5x + 3)$ *[1 mark]*
   $9x + 12 = 10x + 6$ *[1 mark]*
   $12 = x + 6$ so $x = 6$ *[1 mark]*
   [3 marks available in total — as above]

2. American: $12.99 = \dfrac{12.99}{1.43} = £9.0839... = £9.08$ *[1 mark]*
   French: €10.99 = 10.99 × 0.81 = £8.9019 = £8.90 *[1 mark]*
   British: £8.99
   The French website is the cheapest. *[1 mark]*
   [3 marks available in total — as above]

3. a) $5.4 \leq w < 5.5$
   [2 marks available — 2 marks for the correct answer, otherwise 1 mark for the correct bounds]
   b) The minimum value for the length is 12.25 m. *[1 mark]*
   The minimum area is 12.25 × 5.4 *[1 mark]*
   = 66.15 m² *[1 mark]*
   [3 marks available in total — as above]

4. Shop A: 160 × 1.25 = 200 sticky notes for £2.65.
   He would need to buy 14 boxes to get at least 2700 sticky notes (14 × 200 = 2800). 14 × £2.65 = £37.10
   Shop B: Harold would need to buy 17 boxes to get at least 2700 sticky notes (17 × 160 = 2720). Every other box will be half price, so 9 boxes will be full price and 8 boxes will be half price. (9 × £2.98) + (8 × 0.5 × £2.98) = £38.74
   Shop A would give him the best deal.
   [4 marks available — 1 mark for the number of boxes needed from shop A, 1 mark for the number of boxes needed from shop B, 1 mark for the total cost at one shop, 1 mark for the total cost at the other shop and the correct answer]

5. $16^{-\frac{3}{2}} = \dfrac{1}{16^{\frac{3}{2}}} = \dfrac{1}{\sqrt{16}^3} = \dfrac{1}{4^3} = \dfrac{1}{64}$
   [2 marks available — 1 mark for either the square root or the reciprocal, 1 mark for a complete correct solution]

6. a) $2x - 5 < 5x + 4$
   $-5 < 3x + 4$
   $-9 < 3x$ *[1 mark]*
   $-3 < x$, which can be rewritten as $x > -3$ *[1 mark]*
   [2 marks available in total — as above]
   b) 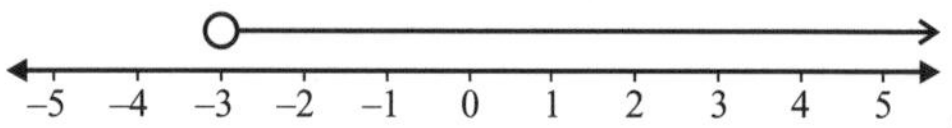

   –5 –4 –3 –2 –1 0 1 2 3 4 5 *[1 mark]*
   Make sure you've only drawn the outline of a circle, as this means that 3 isn't included.

7. a) x = exterior angle = $\dfrac{360}{16}$ = 22.5° *[1 mark]*
   b) 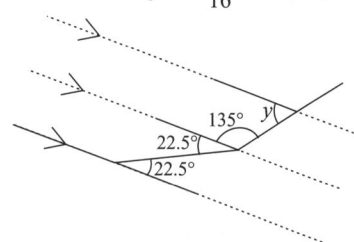 Angle in z-shape = 22.5° (alternate angles)
   Interior angle = 180° – 22.5° = 157.5°
   157.5° – 22.5° = 135°
   y = 180° – 135° = 45° (allied angles)
   [2 marks available — 2 marks for correct answer, otherwise 1 mark for attempt at using angle rules or finding the interior angle]

8. a) In 2015, $t = 0$ so $P = 8000 \times 0.93^0$
   = 8000 × 1 = 8000 *[1 mark]*
   b) In 2018, $t = 3$ and $P = 8000 \times 0.93^3 = 6434.856$
   = 6435 (nearest whole number).
   [2 marks available — 1 mark for the correct substitution of $t = 3$ into the formula, 1 mark for the correct answer]
   c) $t = 4$, $P = 8000 \times 0.93^4 = 5984.4160...$
   $t = 5$, $P = 8000 \times 0.93^5 = 5565.5069...$
   $t = 6$, $P = 8000 \times 0.93^6 = 5175.9214...$
   $t = 7$, $P = 8000 \times 0.93^7 = 4813.6069...$
   So the population is below 5000 after $t = 7$ years.
   [2 marks available — 1 mark for at least two trials, 1 mark for the correct answer]

9. $m\mathbf{a} + n\mathbf{b} = m\begin{pmatrix}2\\-1\end{pmatrix} + n\begin{pmatrix}5\\3\end{pmatrix} = \begin{pmatrix}2m + 5n\\-m + 3n\end{pmatrix} = \begin{pmatrix}1\\-6\end{pmatrix}$
   so $2m + 5n = 1$ and $-m + 3n = -6$. *[1 mark]*
   $-m + 3n = -6 \xrightarrow{\times 2} -2m + 6n = -12$ *[1 mark]*
   $-2m + 6n = -12$
   $2m + 5n = 1$ +
   $11n = -11$
   $n = -1$ *[1 mark]*
   $-m + (3 \times -1) = -6$
   $-m - 3 = -6$
   $-m = -3$
   $m = 3$ *[1 mark]*
   [4 marks available in total — as above]

10. 1 hour 45 min = 1.75 hours, so the distance from Carlisle to Preston is 1.75 × 60 = 105 miles. *[1 mark]*
    Total distance = 105 + 23 = 128 miles
    Total time = 1 hour 45 mins + 35 mins
    = 2 hours 20 minutes = $2\dfrac{1}{3}$ hours
    Average speed = $128 \div 2\dfrac{1}{3}$ *[1 mark]* = 54.8571...
    = 55 mph (to the nearest mph) *[1 mark]*
    [3 marks available in total — as above]

11. a) P(scores 1st) = 0.7
    P(scores both) = P(scores 1st) × P(scores 2nd given scores 1st)
    So P(scores 2nd given scores 1st)
    = P(scores both) ÷ P(scores 1st) = 0.56 ÷ 0.7 = 0.8
    P(misses 2nd given scores 1st) = 1 – 0.8 = 0.2
    P(misses 1st) = 1 – 0.7 = 0.3
    P(misses both) = P(misses 1st) × P(misses 2nd given misses 1st)
    So P(misses 2nd given misses 1st)
    = P(misses both) ÷ P(misses 1st) = 0.18 ÷ 0.3 = 0.6
    P(scores 2nd given misses 1st) = 1 – 0.6 = 0.4

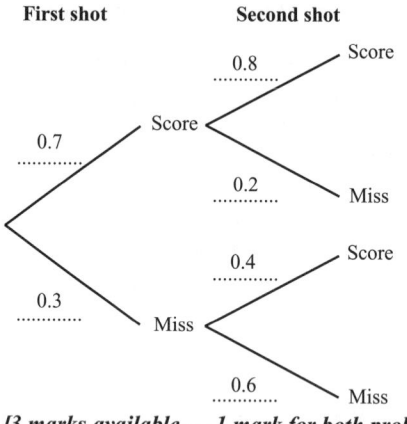

    First shot: 0.7 Score, 0.3 Miss
    Second shot (given Score): 0.8 Score, 0.2 Miss
    Second shot (given Miss): 0.4 Score, 0.6 Miss

    [3 marks available — 1 mark for both probabilities of his first shot, 1 mark for both probabilities for second shot given he scored the first, 1 mark for both probabilities for second shot given he missed the first]
    b) P(misses 1st but scores 2nd) = 0.3 × 0.4 = 0.12 *[1 mark]*
    P(scores 1st but misses 2nd) = 0.7 × 0.2 = 0.14 *[1 mark]*
    Jack is more likely to miss with his second shot. *[1 mark]*
    [3 marks available in total — as above]

14 If x is the multiplier for the annual percentage increase,
then $750 \times x^4 = 844.13$.
$x^4 = \frac{844.13}{750} = 1.1255...$ *[1 mark]*
$x = \sqrt[4]{1.1255...} = 1.0299... = 1.03$ (3 s.f.) *[1 mark]*
So the annual rate of interest was 3%. *[1 mark]*
[3 marks available in total — as above]

15 a) The estimated 32 000 is 107% of the original value, so
$32\,000 \div 107 \times 100 = 29\,906.5420... = 29\,907$ *[1 mark]*
and $32\,000 - 29\,907 = 2093$ *[1 mark]*
[2 marks available in total — as above]

b) 32 000 to the nearest 1000 means the minimum population was 31 500 and the maximum population was 32 499.
$31\,500 \div 107 \times 100 = 29\,439.2523... = 29\,439$
$31\,500 - 29\,439 = 2061$ *[1 mark]*
$32\,499 \div 107 \times 100 = 30\,372.897... = 30\,373$
$32\,499 - 30\,373 = 2126$ *[1 mark]*
$2093 - 2061 = 32$ and $2126 - 2093 = 33$. The estimate for part (a) could be a maximum of 33 away from the actual value, not 500, so Mikko is incorrect. *[1 mark]*
[3 marks available in total — as above]

16 a) Draw a tangent to the curve at $t = 6$ and find the gradient.

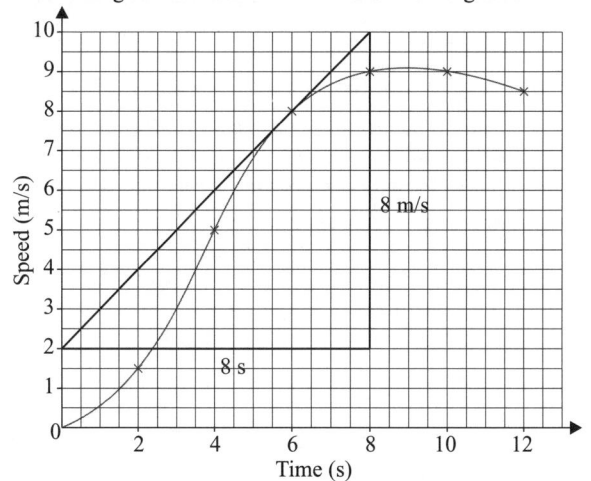

Gradient = acceleration = $\frac{10-2}{8-0} = \frac{8}{8} = 1$ m/s²

[2 marks available — 1 mark for drawing a tangent, 1 mark for an answer in the range 0.8 – 1.2 m/s²]
The accuracy of your tangent will affect the answer you get for the acceleration — award yourself full marks if you're in the range above.

b) Draw 3 equal strips of width 4, and label them A, B and C. Find the area of each strip and add them together.

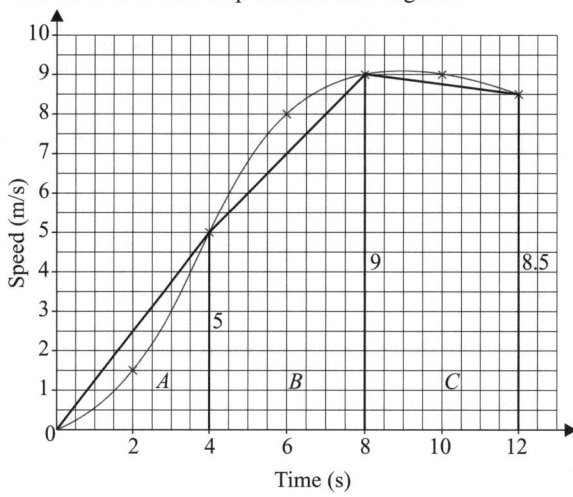

$A = \frac{1}{2} \times 4 \times 5 = 10$ m
$B = \frac{1}{2}(5 + 9) \times 4 = 28$ m
$C = \frac{1}{2}(9 + 8.5) \times 4 = 35$ m
Total distance = $10 + 28 + 35 = 73$ m *[1 mark]*
[3 marks available — 1 mark for drawing 3 strips of width 4 seconds, 1 mark for the correct area of two or more strips, 1 mark for the correct answer]

17 Find the prime factors:
$450 = 2 \times 3^2 \times 5^2$, so $450^3 = (2 \times 3^2 \times 5^2)^3 = 2^3 \times 3^6 \times 5^6$
$240 = 2^4 \times 3 \times 5$, so $240^3 = (2^4 \times 3 \times 5)^3 = 2^{12} \times 3^3 \times 5^3$
Multiply the prime factors that appear in either number:
LCM = $2^{12} \times 3^6 \times 5^6 = (2^2 \times 3 \times 5)^6 = 60^6$
[4 marks available — 1 mark for finding prime factors of 450, 1 mark for finding prime factors of 240, 1 mark for finding the LCM of 450^3 and 240^3, 1 mark for showing the LCM = 60^6]
You can use factor trees to find the prime factors of each number.

18 $6x - 3$ factorises to $3(2x - 1)$ and
$2x^2 + 7x - 4$ factorises to $(x + 4)(2x - 1)$ *[1 mark]*
$x^2 - 16 = (x - 4)(x + 4)$ *[1 mark]*
So, $\frac{6x-3}{2x^2+7x-4} \div \frac{15}{x^2-16}$
$= \frac{3(2x-1)}{(x+4)(2x-1)} \div \frac{15}{(x-4)(x+4)}$
$= \frac{3(2x-1)}{(x+4)(2x-1)} \times \frac{(x-4)(x+4)}{15}$ *[1 mark]*
$= \frac{3(2x-1)}{(x+4)(2x-1)} \times \frac{(x-4)(x+4)}{15}$
$= \frac{3(x-4)}{15} = \frac{x-4}{5}$ *[1 mark]*
[4 marks available in total — as above]

19 Label CD as the height x, and AD as length y.
$x = 6\tan 34° = 4.0470...$ cm *[1 mark]*
Use Pythagoras' theorem to find y:
$4.0470...^2 + y^2 = 5.4^2$, so $y^2 = 5.4^2 - 4.0470...^2 = 12.7813...$
$y = \sqrt{12.7813...} = 3.5751...$ cm *[1 mark]*
Area of triangle $ABC = \frac{1}{2} \times (3.5751... + 6) \times 4.0470...$ *[1 mark]*
$= 19.3754...$ cm² = 19.38 cm² (2 d.p.) *[1 mark]*
[4 marks available in total — as above]

20 $(3n + 2)^2 - 1 = 9n^2 + 12n + 4 - 1 = 9n^2 + 12n + 3$ *[1 mark]*
There is a common factor of 3 *[1 mark]*, so rewrite this expression as $3(3n^2 + 4n + 1)$ which is a multiple of 3 for all positive integers. *[1 mark]*
[3 marks available in total — as above]

21 If radius of shaded circle = r
Area of shaded circle = πr^2 *[1 mark]*
Radius of sector = $2r$
Area of sector = $\frac{360° - a}{360°} \times \pi \times (2r)^2$
$= \frac{360° - a}{360°} \times 4\pi r^2$ *[1 mark]*
Area of shaded circle = 30% of area of sector
$\pi r^2 = 0.3 \times \frac{360° - a}{360°} \times 4\pi r^2$ *[1 mark]*
$1 = 1.2 \times \frac{360° - a}{360°}$
$\frac{360°}{1.2} = 360° - a$
$300° = 360° - a$
$a = 60°$ *[1 mark]*
[4 marks available in total — as above]

6 a) [Venn diagram: ξ rectangle containing two circles M and F. M-only contains 9; overlap contains 3, 6, 12; F-only contains 1, 2, 4, 5, 10; outside circles: 8, 11, 7]

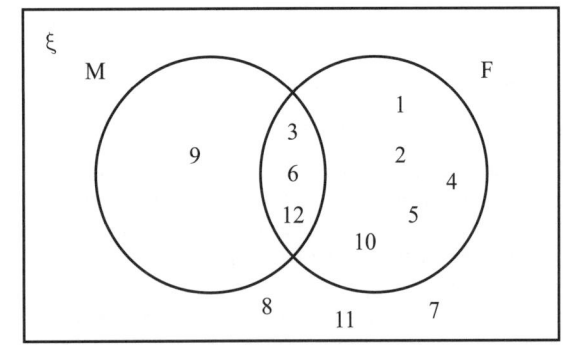

[3 marks available — 1 mark for the correct values in the circles, 1 mark for the correct values in the overlap, 1 mark for correct values outside of the circles]

b) M ∩ F = {3, 6, 12}. There are 12 numbers in total, so P(M ∩ F) = $\frac{3}{12}$ (or $\frac{1}{4}$). *[1 mark]*

(M ∪ F)' = {7, 8, 11} so P(M ∪ F)' = $\frac{3}{12}$ (or $\frac{1}{4}$). *[1 mark]*

[2 marks available in total — as above]
If you've stated that the probability is equal as the set M ∩ F has the same number of elements as the set (M ∪ F)' you'll still get the marks.

7 a) g(–2) = (–2)^2 – 3 = 4 – 3 = 1 *[1 mark]*

b) Set $x = 3y - 5$, and rearrange to make y the subject.
$3y = x + 5$
$y = \frac{x+5}{3}$
So $f^{-1}(x) = \frac{x+5}{3}$

[2 marks available — 1 mark for the correct method, 1 mark for the correct answer]

c) gf(x) = g(3x – 5)
g(3x – 5) = (3x – 5)^2 – 3 *[1 mark]*
= 9x^2 – 30x + 25 – 3 = 9x^2 – 30x + 22 *[1 mark]*
[2 marks available in total — as above]

8 a) 60% of 30 = 0.6 × 30 = 18 attended revision class.
30 – 18 = 12 did not attend revision class.
18 – 15 = 3 attended but did not achieve target grade.
30 × $\frac{2}{3}$ = 20 in total achieved target grade.
20 – 15 = 5 did not attend but achieved target grade.
12 – 5 = 7 did not attend and did not achieve target grade.

[Tree diagram: 30 branches to "attended revision class" (18) → "achieved target grade" (15), "did not achieve target grade" (3); and "did not attend revision class" (12) → "achieved target grade" (5), "did not achieve target grade" (7)]

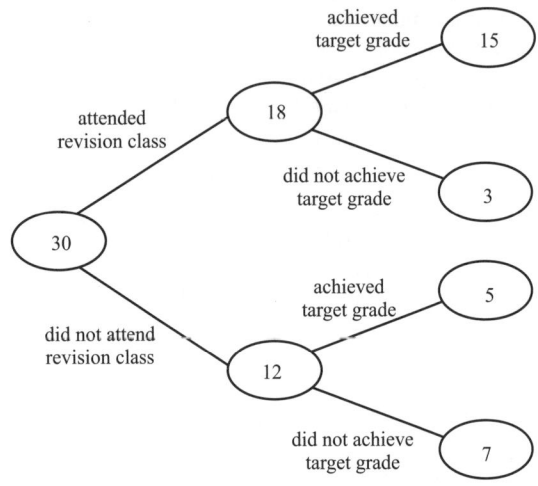

[3 marks available — 3 marks for tree fully correct, otherwise 2 marks if one value is incorrect, or 1 mark if two values are incorrect]
Check you haven't made any mistakes by checking each 'column' of numbers adds to the same number (30 in this case).

b) There are 12 students who didn't go to revision class and 5 achieved their target grade so the probability is $\frac{5}{12}$.
[1 mark]

9 $c \propto a^2$, so $c = ka^2$.
When $a = 10$, $c = 1500$ so $1500 = k \times 10^2 = 100k$.
So, $k = 15$ and $c = 15a^2$ *[1 mark]*
When $c = 2940$, $2940 = 15a^2$
$a^2 = 196$ *[1 mark]*
$a = 14$ *[1 mark]*
[3 marks available in total — as above]

10 d is the exterior angle of a regular pentagon, so
$d = 360° \div 5 = 72°$. *[1 mark]*
The triangle is isosceles, so the unmarked angle is also 72°.
$c = 180° - 72° - 72° = 36°$ *[1 mark]*
The ratio $c:d$ is 36:72 which simplifies to 1:2. *[1 mark]*
[3 marks available in total — as above]

11 a) 30 cm = 0.3 m
$T = 2\pi \times \sqrt{\frac{0.3}{9.78}} = 1.1004... = 1.10$ (3 s.f) seconds
[2 marks available — 1 mark for using 0.3 in the formula, 1 mark for the correct answer]
Make sure that you check all measurements have the correct units before putting them into a formula.

b) The change in T from the Equator to the North Pole is
$2\pi \times \sqrt{\frac{0.3}{9.78}} - 2\pi \times \sqrt{\frac{0.3}{9.832}} = 0.002913...$ seconds
The percentage change is
$\frac{0.002913...}{1.1004...} \times 100 = 0.2647...\% = 0.265\%$ (3 s.f.)
[3 marks available — 1 mark for finding the difference between the two periods, 1 mark for using the percentage change formula, 1 mark for the correct answer]

12 a) Minimum = 8, maximum = 24
Median = (11 + 1) ÷ 2 = 6th value = 15
Lower quartile = (11 + 1) ÷ 4 = 3rd value = 11
Upper quartile = 3(11 + 1) ÷ 4 = 9th value = 19

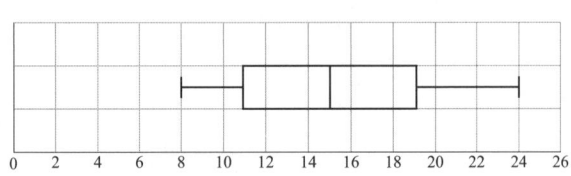

[Box plot on scale 0 to 26 with minimum at 8, LQ at 11, median at 15, UQ at 19, maximum at 24]

[3 marks available — 1 mark for correctly plotting the minimum and maximum values, 1 mark for correctly plotting the lower and upper quartiles, 1 mark for correctly plotting the median]

b) E.g. On average the students scored higher marks in the chemistry exam than the physics exam, as the median is higher for chemistry. The students' marks on the chemistry exam were more spread out (inconsistent) as the range and interquartile range are both larger.
[2 marks available — 1 mark for comparing the average marks with a correct conclusion, 1 mark for comparing the spread of marks with a correct conclusion]

13 The gradient of the line from (2, 7) to (5, 13) = $\frac{13-7}{5-2} = \frac{6}{3} = 2$
[1 mark]
Two lines are perpendicular if their gradients multiply to equal –1, so a perpendicular line to 2 will have a gradient of $-\frac{1}{2}$.
[1 mark]
The equation $2y = 13 - x$ can be rearranged to give $y = \frac{13}{2} - \frac{1}{2}x$.
The gradient is $-\frac{1}{2}$ and so the two lines are perpendicular.
[1 mark]
[3 marks available in total — as above]

17 Area of circle = πr^2
Area of entire circle = $\pi \times 11^2 = 121\pi$
Area of inner two circles (grey and white) = $\pi \times (5 + 2)^2 = 49\pi$
Area of innermost grey circle = $\pi \times 5^2 = 25\pi$
Shaded area of entire circle = $121\pi - 49\pi + 25\pi = 97\pi$
Area of shaded sector = $\frac{120}{360} \times 97\pi = \frac{1}{3} \times 97\pi = \frac{97}{3}\pi$
[4 marks available — 1 mark for finding the area of the entire circle, 1 mark for finding the area of one of the inner circles, 1 mark for the shaded area of the entire circle, 1 mark for the correct answer]

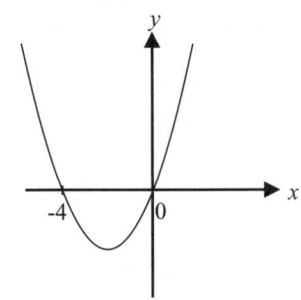

18 a) *[2 marks available — 1 mark for correct intercepts (–4, 0) and (0, 0), 1 mark for correctly drawn graph]*

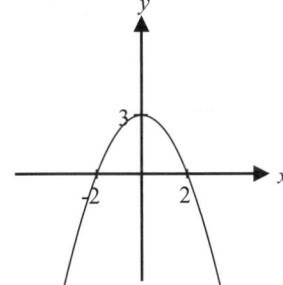

b) *[2 marks available — 1 mark for correct intercepts (–2, 0), (2, 0) and (0, 3), 1 mark for correctly drawn graph]*

19 $\sin 60° = \frac{\sqrt{3}}{2}$ *[1 mark]* $\tan 30° = \frac{1}{\sqrt{3}}$ *[1 mark]*
$2 \times \frac{\sqrt{3}}{2} \times \frac{1}{\sqrt{3}} = \frac{2\sqrt{3}}{2\sqrt{3}} = 1$ *[1 mark]*
[3 marks available in total — as above]

20 a) $-\frac{6}{2} = -3$, so $a = -3$, $(x - 3)^2 = x^2 - 6x + 9$
so $b = -11$ and $x^2 - 6x - 2 = (x - 3)^2 - 11$
[2 marks available — 1 mark for the correct value of a, 1 mark for the correct value of b]

b) (3, –11) *[1 mark]*

21 To prove all triangles are similar, show that the angles are the same in each triangle. Let angle $ABC = x$, then
Triangle ABC contains:
Angle $BCA = 90°$ (as the angle in a semicircle is 90°)
Angle $ABC = x$, and angle $BAC = 180° - 90° - x = 90° - x$
Triangle ABD contains:
Angle $DAB = 90°$ (as angle where a tangent meets a radius is 90°)
Angle ABD = angle $ABC = x$ and
Angle $ADB = 180° - 90° - x = 90° - x$
Triangle ACD contains:
Angle $ACD = 180°$ – angle $BCA = 180° - 90° = 90°$
Angle ADC = angle $ADB = 90° - x$
Angle $DAC = 180° - 90° - (90° - x) = x$
The three angles in all triangles are 90°, x and (90° – x) so all three triangles are similar.
[4 marks available — 1 mark for finding the angles in triangle ABC, 1 mark for finding the angles in triangle ABD, 1 mark for finding the angles in triangle ACD, 1 mark for a conclusion that all triangles contain same angles so are similar]

22 $c + 3 : a + 3 = 2 : 3$
$\frac{c+3}{a+3} = \frac{2}{3}$, so $3(c + 3) = 2(a + 3)$
$3c + 9 = 2a + 6$
$3c - 2a = -3$ *[1 mark]*

$c + 1 : a + 5 = 1 : 2$
$\frac{c+1}{a+5} = \frac{1}{2}$, so $2(c + 1) = a + 5$
$2c + 2 = a + 5$
$2c - a = 3$ *[1 mark]*

$2c - a = 3 \xrightarrow{\times 2} 4c - 2a = 6$ *[1 mark]*

$3c - 2a = -3$
$- \quad 4c - 2a = 6$
$\overline{-c = -9}$
$c = 9$ *[1 mark]*

$2c - a = 3$
$2 \times 9 - a = 3$
$18 - a = 3$
$a = 15$ *[1 mark]*

The ratio $c : a = 9 : 15 = 3 : 5$ in its simplest terms. *[1 mark]*
[6 marks available in total — as above]

Set 2 Paper 2 — Calculator

1 $7 \times 4 \times 5 = 140$ choices *[1 mark]*
$140 \times £3.50 = £490$ *[1 mark]*
[2 marks available in total — as above]

2 1 fathom = 1.8 m
1.782 km = 1.782 × 1000 = 1782 m *[1 mark]*
1782 m = 1782 ÷ 1.8 = 990 fathoms *[1 mark]*
[2 marks available in total — as above]

3 a) E.g.
The number of people using the site grew slowly between 2007 and 2009, then increased at a steady rate between 2009 and 2012. *[1 mark]*
The number of people increased more slowly between 2012 and 2014. *[1 mark]*
[2 marks available in total — as above]

b) E.g. The graph suggests there could be 125 000 people using the website by 2017. This is unreliable because the trend may change as 2017 is outside the data that is available, and there may be a sharp increase or decrease in the number of users.
[2 marks available — 1 mark for a prediction between 120 000 to 130 000, 1 mark for a correct point on reliability]
You could argue that the graph is reliable as it shows a smooth curve which may continue past the data points.

4 The values in the two ratios that represent 'milk' are 3 and 7.
21 is the lowest common multiple of 3 and 7, so multiply the first ratio by 7 to get 14:21, and the second ratio by 3 to get 21:6 *[1 mark]*
So, the ratio of all three chocolates is 14:21:6 *[1 mark]*
There are 14 + 21 + 6 = 41 parts,
So one part is 123 ÷ 41 = 3 chocolates
There are 14 × 3 = 42 plain chocolates *[1 mark]*
[3 marks available in total — as above]

5 a) The difference between each term is 7, so the expression for the nth term will include a $7n$. *[1 mark]*
The sequence $7n$ is: 7, 14, 21, 28...
Each term in the given arithmetic sequence is 4 less than this sequence, so the nth term = $7n - 4$ *[1 mark]*
[2 marks available in total — as above]

b) If 1024 was in the sequence then $7n - 4 = 1024$ for some integer n. Rearrange to get $7n = 1028$ *[1 mark]*, then $n = 146.8571...$
n is not an integer, so 1028 is not a term of the sequence.
[1 mark]
[2 marks available in total — as above]

7   Prime numbers: 2, 3, 5, 7
    P(throwing prime number on 6-sided dice) = $\frac{3}{6} = \frac{1}{2}$ *[1 mark]*
    P(throwing prime number on 10-sided dice) = $\frac{4}{10} = \frac{2}{5}$ *[1 mark]*
    $\frac{1}{2} \times 300 = 150$, $\frac{2}{5} \times 200 = 80$
    So an estimated 150 + 80 = 230 prime numbers will be rolled.
    [1 mark]
    [3 marks available in total — as above]

8   Any two valid reasons, e.g.
    • Mesut's results do not include anyone under the age of 12.
    • He also only asked people at one time of day, on a Monday.
    [2 marks available — 1 mark for each correct reason]

9   45 mph ≈ 45 ÷ 5 × 8 = 72 km per hour
    = 72 000 m per hour *[1 mark]*
    72 000 m per hour = $\frac{72\,000}{60 \times 60} = \frac{72\,000}{3600}$ m/s *[1 mark]*
    $\frac{72\,000}{3600} = 20$ m/s *[1 mark]*
    [3 marks available in total — as above]

10 a) 1 bricklayer can lay $\frac{3000}{5} = 600$ bricks per day, so
        3 bricklayers can lay 3 × 600 = 1800 bricks per day. *[1 mark]*
        They could lay the bricks for one bungalow in
        5400 ÷ 1800 = 3 days *[1 mark]*
        So for 20 bungalows it would take 3 × 20 = 60 days *[1 mark]*
        [3 marks available in total — as above]
    b) Any two valid assumptions, e.g.
        • The bricklayers all lay bricks at the same rate as Scott.
        • The bricklayers work as quickly together as they do separately.
        • Each bungalow uses roughly the same number of bricks.
        [2 marks available — 1 mark for each correct assumption]

11 $2y = \frac{3x}{2-5x}$
    $2y(2 - 5x) = 3x$ *[1 mark]*
    $4y - 10xy = 3x$
    $4y = 3x + 10xy$ *[1 mark]*
    $4y = x(3 + 10y)$
    $x = \frac{4y}{3 + 10y}$ *[1 mark]*
    [3 marks available in total — as above]

12 Distance travelled in first 6 days is 6 × 5.5 = 33 miles. *[1 mark]*
    Distance travelled in 7 days = 7 × 6 = 42 miles. *[1 mark]*
    So Jen travelled 42 – 33 = 9 miles on the 7th day. *[1 mark]*
    [3 marks available in total — as above]

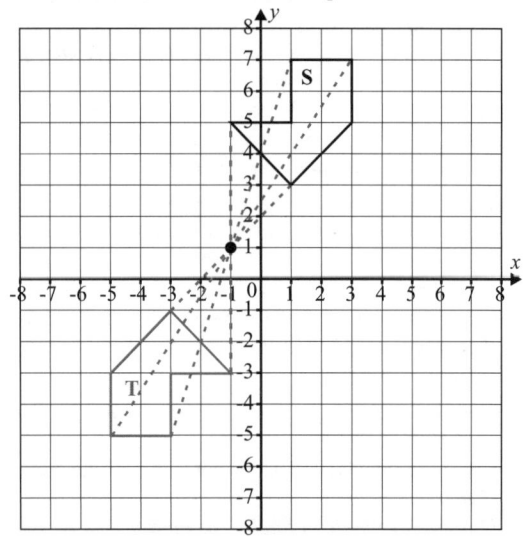

13 a) *[2 marks available — 1 mark for shape drawn with correct scale factor of 1 (in any orientation), 1 mark for enlargement fully correct]*

    b) Rotation of 180° *[1 mark]* about point (–1, 1) *[1 mark]*
        [2 marks available in total — as above]

14 $\frac{3.2 \times 10^4}{8 \times 10^{-2}} = \frac{32 \times 10^3}{8 \times 10^{-2}}$ *[1 mark]*
    $= \frac{32}{8} \times \frac{10^3}{10^{-2}} = 4 \times 10^3 \times 10^2 = 4 \times 10^5$ *[1 mark]*
    [2 marks available in total — as above]
    Alternatively you could have found that (3.2 × 10⁴) ÷ (8 × 10⁻²) = 0.4 × 10⁶ and then converted this answer into standard form.

15 Work out which side of each line should be shaded:
    $x \geq 1$: Shade the side where x is greater than 1,
              which is the side that doesn't contain the origin.
    $y \geq x - 1$: x = 0, y = 0 gives 0 ≥ –1, which is true,
              so shade the side containing the origin.
    $2y + x \leq 8$: x = 0, y = 0 gives 0 ≤ 8, which is true,
              so shade the side containing the origin.

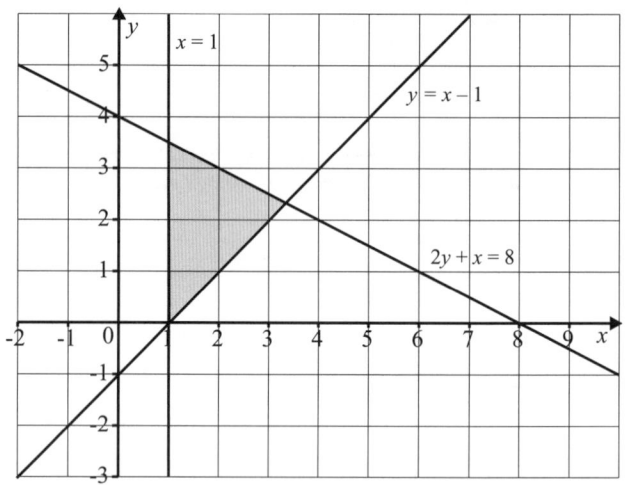

    [4 marks available — 1 mark for each line drawn correctly, 1 mark for shading the correct region]

16 a) $\sin a = \frac{\text{opp}}{\text{hyp}} = \frac{3}{2\sqrt{6}}$. Draw any triangle where the hypotenuse and opposite side are in this ratio. E.g.

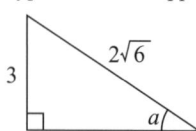

        Use Pythagoras to find the side adjacent to a.
        $\text{adj}^2 = (2\sqrt{6})^2 - 3^2$ *[1 mark]* = 24 – 9 = 15
        $\text{adj} = \sqrt{15}$ *[1 mark]*
        So $\tan a = \frac{\text{opp}}{\text{adj}} = \frac{3}{\sqrt{15}}$ *[1 mark]*
        [3 marks available in total — as above]

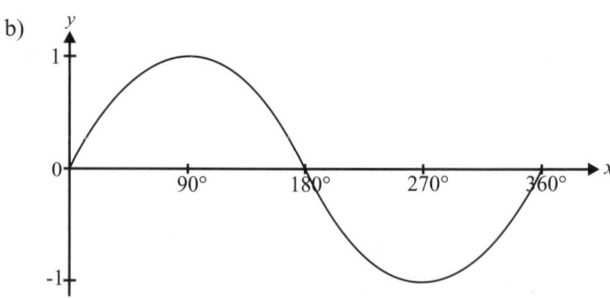

    b) *[2 marks available — 1 mark for correct graph shape, 1 mark for graph passing through points (0°, 0), (90°, 1), (180°, 0), (270°, –1), (360°, 0)]*

    c) For 180° ≤ x ≤ 360° the graph is symmetrical about x = 270°, so x = 180° + 30 = 210° or x = 360° – 30 = 330°
        [2 marks available — 1 mark for each solution for x]

b) x^3 is on the right hand side of the equation, so this suggests to rearrange and make x^2 the subject.
$x^3 + 4x^2 - 13 = 0$
$4x^2 = 13 - x^3$ *[1 mark]*
$x^2 = \frac{13 - x^3}{4}$ so $x = \sqrt{\frac{13 - x^3}{4}}$ *[1 mark]*
[2 marks available in total — as above]

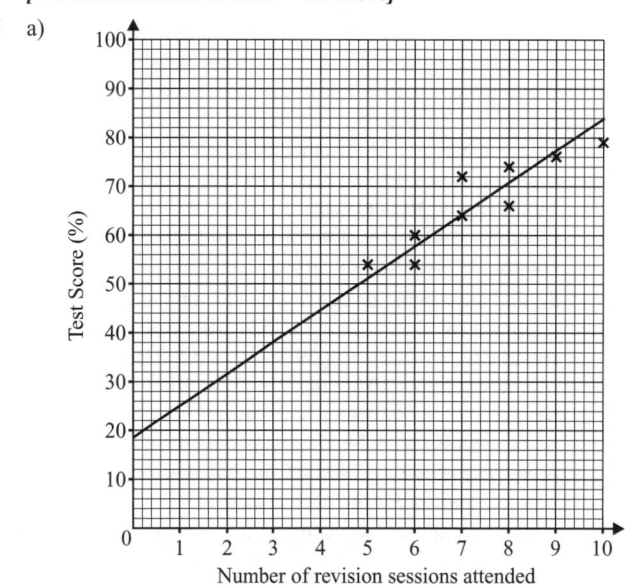

c) Substitute successive values back into the same formula. You can do this using the Ans button on your calculator.
Type $\sqrt{\frac{13 - \text{Ans}^3}{4}}$ and press = until you get to the required level of accuracy. Remember to write down each iteration:

x_0	1.5
x_1	1.5512...
x_2	1.5221...
x_3	1.5389...
x_4	1.5293...
x_5	1.5348...

x_4 and x_5 both round to the same number to 2 d.p. so $x = 1.53$ (to 2 d.p.)
[3 marks available — 1 mark for 1 correct iteration, 1 mark for 5 correct iterations, 1 mark for the correct answer]

19 a) Let E be the centre of base $ABCD$.
The vertical height of the pyramid is the same as the height of the triangle OAE or OAC.
Work out the length AE by using Pythagoras' theorem.
$AE^2 = 4^2 + 4^2 = 32$
$AE = \sqrt{32}$ cm *[1 mark]*
Work out the height OE using Pythagoras' theorem.
$OE^2 = OA^2 - AE^2 = 12^2 - 32 = 144 - 32 = 112$
$OE = \sqrt{112}$ cm *[1 mark]*
$= \sqrt{16}\sqrt{7} = 4\sqrt{7}$ cm *[1 mark]*
[3 marks available in total — as above]

b) The angle required is angle OAE. Call it x.
$\tan x = \frac{OE}{AE} = \frac{4\sqrt{7}}{\sqrt{32}}$ *[1 mark]*
$x = \tan^{-1}\left(\frac{4\sqrt{7}}{\sqrt{32}}\right)$ *[1 mark]* $= 61.8744...°$
$= 61.9°$ (3 s.f.) *[1 mark]*
[3 marks available in total — as above]
You could also have used cos or sin to get the correct answer.

20 a) P(red) = r so P(blue) = $1 - r$
P(exactly 1 red) = P(red, blue) + P(blue, red)
$= r \times (1 - r) + (1 - r) \times r = 2r(1 - r)$ *[1 mark]*
So $2r(1 - r) = \frac{4}{9}$
$2r - 2r^2 = \frac{4}{9}$
$18r - 18r^2 = 4$
$18r^2 - 18r + 4 = 0$ *[1 mark]*
$9r^2 - 9r + 2 = 0$
$(3r - 1)(3r - 2) = 0$ *[1 mark]*
$r = \frac{1}{3}$ or $r = \frac{2}{3}$ *[1 mark]*
[4 marks available in total — as above]
If you're struggling to make an equation for r, you could use a tree diagram to help you find P(exactly 1 red).

b) The ratio of red beads to blue beads is $\frac{1}{3} : \frac{2}{3}$ (or $\frac{2}{3} : \frac{1}{3}$)
$= 1 : 2$ (or $2 : 1$). So there are twice as many of one coloured bead than the other.
Isaac is not correct, as there can't be an odd number of both red beads and blue beads, as odd × 2 = even, and even × 2 = even
[2 marks available — 1 mark for saying that there are twice as many of one coloured bead than the other, 1 mark for a correct conclusion]

Set 2 Paper 1 — Non-calculator

1   $85.6 \div 0.4 = 856 \div 4$
214
$4\overline{|8\ 5^16}$ so $85.6 \div 0.4 = 214$
[2 marks available — 1 mark for a correct method, 1 mark for the correct answer]

2   $3\frac{1}{4} = \frac{13}{4}$ and $1\frac{3}{5} = \frac{8}{5}$ *[1 mark]*
$3\frac{1}{4} \times 1\frac{3}{5} = \frac{13}{4} \times \frac{8}{5} = \frac{104}{20}$ *[1 mark]*
$= \frac{26}{5} = 5\frac{1}{5}$ *[1 mark]*
[3 marks available in total — as above]

3 a) $\frac{96}{75} = \frac{32}{25} = \frac{128}{100} = 128\%$
[2 marks available — 1 mark for a correct method, 1 mark for the correct answer]

b) 10% of 60 = 60 ÷ 10 = 6
1% of 60 = 6 ÷ 10 = 0.6
12% of 60 = 6 + 0.6 + 0.6 = 7.2 *[1 mark]*
60 + 7.2 = 67.2 *[1 mark]*
[2 marks available in total — as above]

4   3 + 2 = 5, so there are 5 parts. 1 part $= \frac{14}{5} = 2.8$ *[1 mark]*
3 parts = 2.8 × 3 = 8.4, so the maximum number of boys is 8.
[1 mark]
[2 marks available in total — as above]

5 a) [graph of Test Score (%) vs Number of revision sessions attended with line of best fit]
[1 mark for appropriate line of best fit]

b) There is a positive correlation — the more revision sessions attended, the higher the test score. *[1 mark]*

c) E.g. The teacher's statement is unreliable because the teacher is making her claim based on using a line of best fit extended a long way from the range of the collected data.
[2 marks available — 1 mark for saying that the teacher's statement is unreliable, 1 mark for a correct explanation]

6 a) $392 = 2 \times 2 \times 2 \times 7 \times 7 = 2^3 \times 7^2$
[3 marks available — 1 mark for 2 × 2 × 2, 1 mark for 7 × 7, 1 mark for $2^3 \times 7^2$]
If you're struggling to find prime factors, try using a factor tree.

b) The common prime factors of 126 and 392 are 2 and 7, so the highest common factor is 2 × 7 = 14. *[1 mark]*

c) $126 = 2 \times 3 \times 3 \times 7$ so to make this a square number you need to multiply by 2 × 7 to give:
$2 \times 2 \times 3 \times 3 \times 7 \times 7 = (2 \times 3 \times 7)^2$.
So $k = 2 \times 7 = 14$ *[1 mark]*

10 Consider the upper and lower bound for each measurement by adding or subtracting half of the rounding unit.
400 m: upper bound = 400 + 0.5 = 400.5 m
        lower bound = 400 − 0.5 = 399.5 m *[1 mark]*
64.5 s: upper bound = 64.5 + 0.25 = 64.75 s *[1 mark]*
        lower bound = 64.5 − 0.25 = 64.25 s

Speed = $\frac{distance}{time}$

To get a lower bound on speed, calculate $\frac{\text{lower bound distance}}{\text{upper bound time}}$

= $\frac{399.5}{64.75}$ = 6.1698... = 6.17 m/s (3 s.f.) *[1 mark]*

[3 marks available in total — as above]

11 Volume = $\frac{\pi \times (1.2)^2 \times 4.3}{3}$ = 6.4842... cm³ *[1 mark]*

Density = $\frac{17.5}{6.4842...}$ *[1 mark]* = 2.7 g/cm³ (2 d.p.) *[1 mark]*

[3 marks available in total — as above]

12 Exterior angle = 180° − interior angle = 180° − 160° = 20°
Use the formula: exterior angle = $\frac{360°}{\text{number of sides}}$
Rearrange to get: number of sides = $\frac{360°}{\text{exterior angle}}$
n = $\frac{360°}{20°}$ = 18 sides *[1 mark]*, so 4n = 4 × 18 = 72 sides
Exterior angle (72 sides) = $\frac{360°}{72°}$ = 5° *[1 mark]*
Interior angle (72 sides) = 180° − 5° = 175° *[1 mark]*
[3 marks available in total — as above]

13 a) To find which two countries are closest in terms of population, make all numbers the same power of 10.
Austria: 8.67 × 10⁶ = 0.867 × 10⁷
Compare 3.26, 0.867, 3.33 and 3.05
3.33 − 3.26 = 0.07 is the smallest difference,
so the countries that have the closest population are Morocco and Afghanistan.
[2 marks available — 1 mark for comparing populations, 1 mark for the correct answer]

    b) To find the population density, divide population by area.
Afghanistan: (3.26 × 10⁷) ÷ (6.52 × 10⁵) = 50
Austria: (8.67 × 10⁶) ÷ (8.39 × 10⁴) = 103.3373...
Morocco: (3.33 × 10⁷) ÷ (4.47 × 10⁵) = 74.4966...
Malaysia: (3.05 × 10⁷) ÷ (3.30 × 10⁵) = 92.4242...
So the country with the greatest population density is Austria.
[2 marks available — 1 mark for 2 or more calculations correct, 1 mark for the correct answer]

14 a) A decrease of 24% means the height is 100% − 24% = 76%
= 0.76 *[1 mark]* of the height before the bounce.
Using the compound decay formula:
140 × 0.76⁵ *[1 mark]* = 35.4973... = 35.5 cm (1 d.p.) *[1 mark]*
[3 marks available in total — as above]

    b) Use your formula to find the lowest value of t that gives an answer less than 10.
140 × 0.76⁹ = 11.8426... and 140 × 0.76¹⁰ = 9.000...
t = 10, so it will take 10 bounces.
[2 marks available — 1 mark for calculating t = 9 or t = 10, 1 mark for the correct answer]

15 a) First, work out the area for the top and side of one table.
The top is a circle with radius 90 ÷ 2 = 45 cm = 0.45 m.
The edge is a rectangle with length equal to the circumference of the top and width 3 cm = 0.03 m.
Area of circle = $\pi \times r^2 = \pi \times 0.45^2$ = 0.6361... m² *[1 mark]*
Area of side = ($\pi \times 0.90$) × 0.03 = 0.0848... m² *[1 mark]*
Paint required for one table (2 coats):
= 2 × (0.6361... + 0.0848...) = 1.4419... m² *[1 mark]*
Paint required for 20 tables
= 20 × 1.4419... = 28.8398... m² *[1 mark]*
His tin of paint can cover 12 × 2.5 = 30 m², so he can paint all of the tables with it. *[1 mark]*
[5 marks available in total — as above]

    b) E.g. No paint is wasted from spillage / washing brushes etc.
Tables need exactly two coats of paint.
[1 mark for any suitable assumption]

16 a) 12 ≤ m < 15 bar has height 8 and frequency 3 × 8 = 24.
20 ≤ m < 25 bar has height 3.6 and frequency 5 × 3.6 = 18.

Time (m) in minutes	Frequency
10 ≤ m < 12	8
12 ≤ m < 15	24
15 ≤ m < 20	30
20 ≤ m < 25	18
25 ≤ m < 40	30

10 ≤ m < 12 bar has width 12 − 10 = 2 and height = $\frac{8}{2}$ = 4
25 ≤ m < 40 bar has width 40 − 25 = 15 and height = $\frac{30}{15}$ = 2

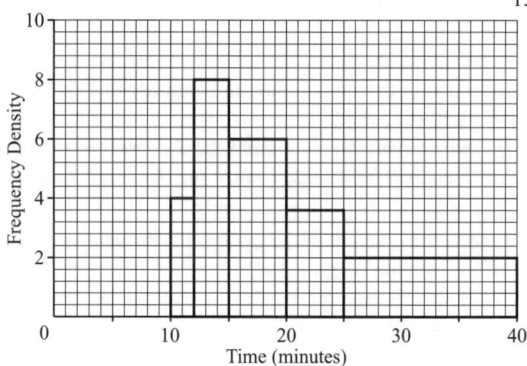

[4 marks available in total — 1 mark for each correct entry in the frequency table, 1 mark for each bar drawn correctly on the histogram]

    b) The quickest competitors completed the fun run in under 12 minutes.
12 minutes = $\frac{12}{60}$ = $\frac{1}{5}$ = 0.2 hours.
speed = $\frac{distance}{time}$, so a competitor who completed the race in 12 minutes would have run at an average speed of
$\frac{10}{0.2}$ = 50 km/h.
This is an impossible pace for humans to run at, so he is not telling the truth.
[2 marks in total — 1 mark for 'not telling the truth', 1 mark for a suitable explanation]

17 a) x^2 − 1 ≤ 3(x + 3)
x^2 − 1 ≤ 3x + 9
x^2 − 3x − 10 ≤ 0 *[1 mark]*
Factorise to (x − 5)(x + 2) = 0.
So, x = 5 and x = −2 are the critical values. *[1 mark]*
Use a value in between the critical values to check if it is in the range of the inequality. *[1 mark]*
If x = 0, x^2 − 3x − 10 = 0² − (3 × 0) − 10 = −10
−10 ≤ 0, so x = 0 is a solution which means the inequality is −2 ≤ x ≤ 5 *[1 mark]*
[4 marks available in total — as above]

    b)
```
●────────────────●
-2      0       5
```
[1 mark]

18 a) If there is a solution between x = 1 and x = 2, you should be able to choose values of x between 1 and 2 such that you get a negative answer and a positive answer.
(1)³ + 4(1)² − 13 = −8
(2)³ + 4(2)² − 13 = 11
There is a change of sign, so there is a solution between x = 1 and x = 2.
[2 marks available — 1 mark for either correct calculation, 1 mark for a correct explanation]

b) $f(x) = 27$
$2x + 3 = 27$
$2x = 24$ so $x = 12$ *[1 mark]*
To find $f^{-1}(x)$, set $x = 2y + 3$, and rearrange to make y the subject.
$2y = x - 3$
$y = \frac{x-3}{2} = f^{-1}(x) = g(x)$ *[1 mark]*
$g(12) = \frac{12-3}{2} = 4.5$
$gg(12) = \frac{4.5-3}{2} = 0.75$ *[1 mark]*
[3 marks available in total — as above]

20 Angle $BCE = n$ = angle ABC (alternate angles are equal) *[1 mark]*
Angle $AOC = 2 \times$ angle $ABC = 2n$ (angle at the centre is twice the angle at the circumference) *[1 mark]*
Angle DAO and angle $DCO = 90°$ (angle where a tangent and a radius meet is 90°) *[1 mark]*
$y = 360° - 90° - 2n - 90°$ (angles in a quadrilateral add up to 360°) $= 180° - 2n$ *[1 mark]*
[4 marks available in total — as above]
There are many different ways to complete this question. If you used a correct method and explained your reasons you'll still get the marks.

21 $\vec{AC} = \vec{AO} + \vec{OC} = \vec{OC} - \vec{OA} = \mathbf{c} - \mathbf{a}$
$AD:DC = 3:2$ means $\vec{AD} = \frac{3}{5}\vec{AC}$ *[1 mark]*
So $\vec{AD} = \frac{3}{5}(\mathbf{c} - \mathbf{a}) = \frac{3}{5}\mathbf{c} - \frac{3}{5}\mathbf{a}$
$\vec{OD} = \vec{OA} + \vec{AD} = \mathbf{a} + \frac{3}{5}\mathbf{c} - \frac{3}{5}\mathbf{a} = \frac{2}{5}\mathbf{a} + \frac{3}{5}\mathbf{c}$ *[1 mark]*
E is $\frac{2}{3}$ of the way along CB, so
$\vec{OE} = \vec{OC} + \frac{2}{3}\vec{CB} = \mathbf{c} + \frac{2}{3}\mathbf{a}$ *[1 mark]*
If ODE is a straight line $\vec{OE}$ must be a multiple of $\vec{OD}$ so
$\mathbf{c} + \frac{2}{3}\mathbf{a} = k(\frac{2}{5}\mathbf{a} + \frac{3}{5}\mathbf{c})$ for some value of k. *[1 mark]*
Compare coefficients of $\mathbf{c}$ to find k: $\mathbf{c} = \frac{3k}{5}\mathbf{c}$ so $k = \frac{5}{3}$
$k\vec{OD} = \frac{5}{3}(\frac{2}{5}\mathbf{a} + \frac{3}{5}\mathbf{c}) = \frac{2}{3}\mathbf{a} + \mathbf{c} = \vec{OE}$ *[1 mark]*
So ODE is a straight line.
[5 marks available in total — as above]
There are many ways to write vectors, so your answer is bound to look a little different to this. Make sure you explain each step and are consistent with how you use your vectors.

Set 1 Paper 3 — Calculator

1 $n^2 = (2^3 \times 3^2 \times 5)^2 = 2^6 \times 3^4 \times 5^2$ *[1 mark]*

2 a) Sweet potato for 1 person $= 180 \div 4 = 45$ g *[1 mark]*
Sweet potato for 25 people $= 45 \times 25 = 1125$ g *[1 mark]*
She needs $1125 - 500 = 625$ g more sweet potato. *[1 mark]*
[3 marks available in total — as above]

b) Amount of lentils for 1 person $= 100 \div 4 = 25$ g.
For n people, she would need $25 \times n = 25n$ g *[1 mark]*

3 a) $(4, 0) - (-2, -1) = (6, 1)$ so A translated 6 units to the right and 1 unit upwards gives B.
As a column vector, this is $\begin{pmatrix} 6 \\ 1 \end{pmatrix}$ *[1 mark]*

b) C lies in the opposite direction from A than B and AC is half the distance as length AB.
So the column vector is $-\frac{1}{2} \times \begin{pmatrix} 6 \\ 1 \end{pmatrix} = \begin{pmatrix} -3 \\ -\frac{1}{2} \end{pmatrix}$ *[1 mark]*

4 1800 pesos $\div 126 \times 5 = £71.4285...$ *[1 mark]*
So the camera is cheaper in Mexico *[1 mark]*
by £79.99 − £71.4285... = £8.5614... = £8.56 (2 d.p.) *[1 mark]*
[3 marks available in total — as above]

5 The number of white dots in the given patterns are 4, 7 and 10. The number of white dots increases by 3 each time so the sequence will contain a $3n$ term. The sequence $3n$ is: 3, 6, 9... The number of white dots of each pattern is 1 more than this sequence, so the nth pattern will have $3n + 1$ white dots. *[1 mark]*
The 1000th pattern will have $(3 \times 1000) + 1 = 3001$ white dots. *[1 mark]*
[2 marks available in total — as above]
If you struggled to see a rule for the number of white dots, you might find it helpful to draw the next couple of patterns in the sequence.

6 a) E.g. Two points on the graph are (0, −4) and (3, 5). Draw a straight line through both points.

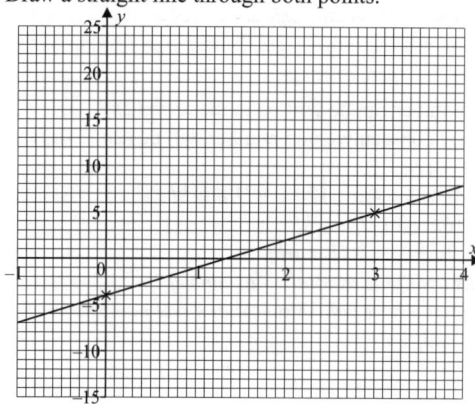

[2 marks available — 1 mark for plotting at least two points accurately, 1 mark for $y = 3x − 4$ drawn correctly]

b) A graph parallel to $y = 3x − 4$ will be in the form $y = 3x + c$.
Substitute in $x = -1$ and $y = 0$
$0 = -3 + c$, so $c = 3$ *[1 mark]*
$y = 3x + 3$ *[1 mark]*
[2 marks available in total — as above]

7 If it is an equilateral triangle then all sides must be equal. Make any 2 sides equal to each other.
$5x − 18 = x + 6$
$4x = 24$ so $x = 6$
Substitute $x = 6$ into each expression:
$PQ = 5 \times 6 − 18 = 12$
$PR = 6 + 6 = 12$
$QR = 3 \times 6 − 5 = 13$
The triangle can't be equilateral because if $PQ = PR$, then QR is not the same length.
[4 marks available — 1 mark for comparing two expressions, 1 mark for finding a value for x, 1 mark for substituting x into the expressions, 1 mark for a correct conclusion]

8 $5 \times (n + 1) \times (n − 1) = 120$ *[1 mark]*
$5 \times (n^2 − n + n − 1) = 120$
$n^2 − 1 = 24$
$n^2 = 25$ so $n = 5$ *[1 mark]*
[2 marks available in total — as above]

9 The mean is 8, so the total must be $4 \times 8 = 32$.
$x + 7 + 13 + y = 32$ so $x + y = 32 − 7 − 13 = 12$. *[1 mark]*
The range is 16, so this is the difference between the largest and smallest number.
Check to see if 13 is the largest number: x is the smallest number so $x = 13 − 16 = −3$, but $x + y = 12$ means $y = 15$, so 13 can't be the largest number.
So y must be the largest number and $y − x = 16$ *[1 mark]*
Add the equations $x + y = 12$ and $y − x = 16$
$x + y + y − x = 12 + 16$
$2y = 28$
$y = 14$ *[1 mark]* and $x = 12 − 14 = −2$ *[1 mark]*
[4 marks available in total — as above]
You can also use trial and error (by trying out different values of x) to get to the correct solution but you must show your working.

b) From the graph, 90 marks gives a cumulative frequency of 60, so there are 80 − 60 = 20 students with a mark of 90 or above.
The ratio 1 : 1.5 = 2 : 3, divides 20 into 20 ÷ 5 × 2 = 8 and 20 ÷ 5 × 3 = 12.
So the top 8 students are awarded a platinum certificate.
The lowest of these is the 73rd person which the graph estimates got 108 marks.
[3 marks available — 1 mark for finding number of students with more than 90 marks, 1 mark for finding number of platinum certificates, 1 mark for an answer in the range of 106-110]
You might get slightly different values in your working, depending on the accuracy of your graph. But your final answer should be within the specified range.

11 An odd number can be written in the form $(2n + 1)$, so the next consecutive odd number will be $(2n + 3)$. *[1 mark]*
$(2n + 1)^2 + (2n + 3)^2$
$= 4n^2 + 4n + 1 + 4n^2 + 12n + 9$ *[1 mark]*
$= 8n^2 + 16n + 10$ *[1 mark]*
$= 8(n^2 + 2n + 1) + 2$ *[1 mark]*
[4 marks available in total — as above]
You could also have written consecutive odd numbers in the form $(2n − 1)$ and $(2n + 1)$.

12 Their current average speed is $\frac{141}{6.75}$ = 20.8888... km/h
The overall required average speed = $\frac{190}{9}$ = 21.1111... km/h
At their current speed they would not make it in time but if they were to increase their speed by a small amount they could make it in the target time.
[2 marks available — 1 mark for comparing the current speed to the required speed, 1 mark for a suitable conclusion]
You could also say that they are more likely to get slower towards the end, so they won't make it in the target time.

13 $\frac{4}{3+\sqrt{5}} + \sqrt{5} = \frac{4+\sqrt{5}(3+\sqrt{5})}{3+\sqrt{5}}$ *[1 mark]*
$= \frac{4+3\sqrt{5}+5}{3+\sqrt{5}} = \frac{9+3\sqrt{5}}{3+\sqrt{5}}$ *[1 mark]*
Take 3 out as a common factor in the numerator and cancel down.
$\frac{3(3+\sqrt{5})}{3+\sqrt{5}} = 3$ *[1 mark]*
[3 marks available in total — as above]
Alternatively, you could multiply the top and bottom of the fraction by $3 − \sqrt{5}$ and then add $\sqrt{5}$ once you've simplified the fraction.

14 a) The difference between each term is 5, so the expression for the nth term will include a $5n$. *[1 mark]*
The sequence $5n$ is: 5, 10, 15, 20, 25...
Each number in the other sequence is 3 more than this sequence, so the nth term = $5n + 3$. *[1 mark]*
[2 marks available — as above]

b) The difference between each term increases by 10, so the expression for the nth term will include a $5n^2$. *[1 mark]*
The sequence $5n^2$ is: 5, 20, 45, 80...
Each number in the other sequence is 8, 13, 18, 23... more than this sequence, which is the same as the sequence from part a), *[1 mark]* so the nth term is $5n^2 + 5n + 3$. *[1 mark]*
[3 marks available in total — as above]

c) Yes, because the second sequence could be written as $5(n^2 + n) + 3$, so both sequences only contain numbers which are a multiple of 5, plus 3. *[1 mark]*

15 a) 6 students study Spanish and German including 4 that study all three languages, so 6 − 4 = 2 students study just Spanish and German.
27 students study Spanish altogether so 27 − 8 − 4 − 2 = 13 students study just Spanish.
There are 50 students altogether, so
50 − (13 + 8 + 4 + 2 + 11 + 3 + 3) = 6 students study no languages.

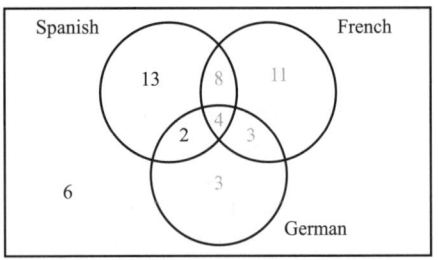

Spanish   French
   13   8   11
        4
     2   3
   6   3
           German

[2 marks available — 1 mark for one or two correct values, 1 mark for all three correct]

b) 13 + 3 + 11 = 27 students study one language. *[1 mark]*
So the probability that one is selected at random is $\frac{27}{50}$ (or 0.54) *[1 mark]*
[2 marks available in total — as above]

c) 8 + 11 + 4 + 3 = 26 students study French. *[1 mark]*
Of these students 8 study Spanish and 3 study German.
So the probability is $\frac{8+3}{26} = \frac{11}{26}$ *[1 mark]*
[2 marks available in total — as above]

16 $y = \frac{k}{\sqrt{x}}$, $12 = \frac{k}{\sqrt{0.09}} = \frac{k}{0.3}$
$k = 12 × 0.3 = 3.6$ *[1 mark]*
When $y = 9$,
$9 = \frac{3.6}{\sqrt{x}}$, $\sqrt{x} = \frac{3.6}{9} = 0.4$ *[1 mark]*
So $x = 0.4^2 = 0.16$ *[1 mark]*
[3 marks available in total — as above]

17 The volumes are in the ratio 1 : 8 so the side lengths are in the ratio $\sqrt[3]{1} : \sqrt[3]{8}$ = 1 : 2 *[1 mark]*
Let R be the radius of the large sphere.
$28 = 4\pi R^2$
$R^2 = \frac{28}{4\pi}$ *[1 mark]*
$R = \sqrt{\frac{7}{\pi}}$ = 1.4927... cm *[1 mark]*
r = 1.4927... ÷ 2 = 0.7463... = 0.75 cm (2 d.p.) *[1 mark]*
[4 marks available in total — as above]

18 $AC = 9 × \sin 42°$ *[1 mark]* = 6.0221... cm *[1 mark]*
Calculate angle ADC using the sine rule:
$\frac{\sin ADC}{6.0221...} = \frac{\sin 49°}{13}$ *[1 mark]*
$\sin ADC = \frac{\sin 49 × 6.0221...}{13} = 0.3496...$
So, angle $ADC = \sin^{-1}(0.3496...) = 20.4637...$
$= 20.5°$ (3 s.f.) *[1 mark]*
[4 marks available in total — as above]

19 a) $(2x + 3)^2 = 5$
$4x^2 + 12x + 9 = 5$
$4x^2 + 12x + 4 = 0$ *[1 mark]*
Use the quadratic formula where $a = 4$, $b = 12$, $c = 4$:
$x = \frac{-12 \pm \sqrt{12^2 - 4 \times 4 \times 4}}{2 \times 4}$ *[1 mark]*
$= \frac{-12 \pm \sqrt{80}}{8}$
$x = -2.62$ (2 d.p.) or $x = -0.38$ (2 d.p.) *[1 mark]*
[3 marks available in total — as above]
You could simplify the quadratic equation to $x^2 + 3x + 1 = 0$ before substituting the values into the quadratic formula.

21 a) Rearrange the linear equation and make x the subject.
$x - 3y = 10$
$x = 3y + 10$
Substitute this equation into $x^2 + y^2 = 20$:
$(3y + 10)^2 + y^2 = 20$ *[1 mark]*
Multiply out the brackets and simplify.
$(3y + 10)^2 + y^2 = 20$
$(3y + 10)(3y + 10) + y^2 = 20$
$9y^2 + 60y + 100 + y^2 = 20$
$10y^2 + 60y + 80 = 0$ *[1 mark]*
Divide through by 10 to get $y^2 + 6y + 8 = 0$
Factorise and solve to find y.
$(y + 2)(y + 4) = 0$ *[1 mark]*
$y = -2$ or $y = -4$
Use $x = 3y + 10$ to find x.
When $y = -2$, $x = (3 \times -2) + 10 = 4$ *[1 mark]*
When $y = -4$, $x = (3 \times -4) + 10 = -2$ *[1 mark]*
[5 marks available in total — as above]
You could have rearranged the linear equation to make y the subject but it's a lot trickier to get to the solution.

b) The graph will have two points of intersection at $(4, -2)$ and $(-2, -4)$, as the simultaneous equations have two solutions.
[1 mark]

22 Work out the coordinates of point A.
$x^2 + y^2 = 5$
$x^2 + (-1)^2 = 5$
$x^2 + 1 = 5$
$x^2 = 4$
$x = 2$ or $x = -2$
A has a positive x-coordinate so has coordinates $(2, -1)$ *[1 mark]*
The tangent at A is perpendicular to the radius drawn to A.
Gradient of radius from $(0, 0)$ to $(2, -1) = \frac{0-(-1)}{0-2} = -\frac{1}{2}$
[1 mark]
Two lines are perpendicular if their gradients multiply to equal -1, so the gradient of the tangent is 2 and has equation $y = 2x + c$. *[1 mark]*
Substitute the coordinates of A to find c.
$-1 = 2(2) + c$
$-1 = 4 + c$
$c = -5$ *[1 mark]*
$y = 2x - 5$, so when $y = 0$, $x = 2.5$ and when $x = 0$, $y = -5$.
So, B has coordinates $(2.5, 0)$ and C has coordinates $(0, -5)$.
Area of triangle $= \frac{1}{2} \times 2.5 \times 5 = 6.25$ or $\frac{25}{4}$ or $6\frac{1}{4}$ *[1 mark]*
[5 marks available in total — as above]

Set 1 Paper 2 — Calculator

1. 1 kg = 1 000 000 mg = 10^6 mg
2.5 mg = $2.5 \div 10^6$ *[1 mark]* = 2.5×10^{-6} kg *[1 mark]*
[2 marks available in total — as above]

2. a) $\frac{12x^4y^3}{2x^3y^7} = \frac{6x}{y^4}$ or $6xy^{-4}$
[2 marks available — 1 mark for correct index for x or y, 1 mark for the correct answer]

b) $3(x - 5) = 5x + 11$
$3x - 15 = 5x + 11$ *[1 mark]*
$-26 = 2x$, so $x = -13$ *[1 mark]*
[2 marks available in total — as above]

3. £11 367 = 3 shares, so 1 share = £11 367 $\div$ 3 = £3789
Alison's share is £3789 $\times$ 7 = £26 523 *[1 mark]*
Che's share is £3789 $\times$ 2 = £7578 *[1 mark]*
Alison gets £26 523 − £7578 = £18 945 more than Che. *[1 mark]*
[3 marks available in total — as above]
There is a difference of $7 - 2 = 5$ shares between Alison and Che, so you could do £3789 $\times$ 5 = £18 945 too.

4. a) $2 - 4x \leq 12$
$2 - 12 \leq 4x$
$-10 \leq 4x$ *[1 mark]*
$-2.5 \leq x$ *[1 mark]*
[2 marks available in total — as above]

b) From part a)(i) $n \geq -2.5$, so the smallest integer value of n is -2. *[1 mark]*

5. a) Work out the LCM of 15 and 18. $15 = 3 \times 5$, $18 = 2 \times 3 \times 3$.
So LCM $= 2 \times 3 \times 3 \times 5 = 90$
90 minutes after 2:00 pm is 3:30 pm
[2 marks available — 1 mark for finding the LCM of 15 and 18, 1 mark for the correct answer]

b) E.g. The buses run exactly on time.
[1 mark for a suitable assumption]

6. Let $x = 0.411111...$
So, $10x = 4.11111...$ and $100x = 41.11111...$ *[1 mark]*
$100x - 10x = 41.11111... - 4.11111...$
$90x = 37$
So, $x = \frac{37}{90}$ *[1 mark]*
[2 marks available in total — as above]

7. a) Take the midpoints of each class, multiply by the frequency and divide by the total.
$(45 \times 27) + (55 \times 30) + (65 \times 16) + (75 \times 7) = 4430$
$27 + 30 + 16 + 7 = 80$
So, the mean mass is $4430 \div 80 = 55.375$ g
[3 marks available — 1 mark for multiplying each midpoint by the corresponding frequency, 1 mark for dividing the sum of the multiplied frequencies by the number of eggs, 1 mark for the correct answer]

b) There are 27 eggs in the $40 \leq m < 50$ class, which all weigh less than 53 g.
Assuming the eggs are evenly distributed within a class, $\frac{53-50}{60-50} = \frac{3}{10}$ of the eggs in the $50 \leq m < 60$ class weigh 53 g or less. *[1 mark]*
$27 + \left(\frac{3}{10} \times 30\right) = 36$ *[1 mark]*
As a percentage, $\frac{36}{80} \times 100 = 45\%$ are small eggs. *[1 mark]*
[3 marks available in total — as above]

8. Using Pythagoras' theorem $7.8^2 + 8.1^2$ must be equal to 12.3^2
$7.8^2 + 8.1^2 = 126.45$ *[1 mark]*
$12.3^2 = 151.29$ *[1 mark]*
$126.45 \neq 151.29$, so the triangle is not right-angled. *[1 mark]*
[3 marks available in total — as above]

9. Arc length $= \frac{150}{360} \times \pi \times (6 \times 2)$ *[1 mark]*
$= \frac{5}{12} \times \pi \times 12 = 5\pi$ cm *[1 mark]*
[2 marks available in total — as above]

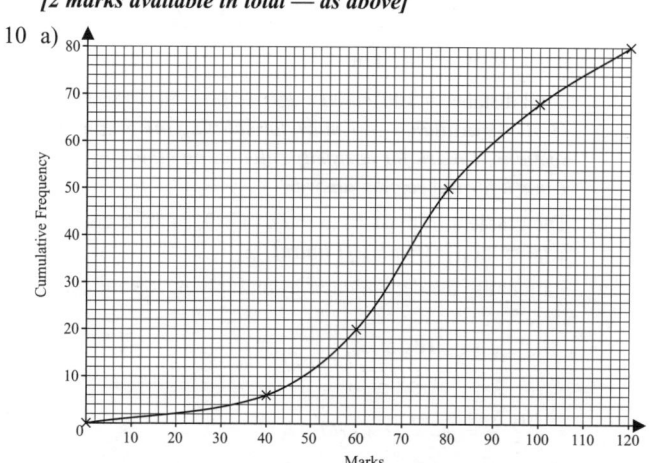

10. a) *[2 marks available — 1 mark for correctly plotting each point, 1 mark for joining points with a smooth curve or with straight lines]*

10 a) $y = x^2$ *[1 mark]*
    b) $y = -2^x$ *[1 mark]*
    c) $y = \frac{1}{x}$ *[1 mark]*
    d) $y = \cos x$ *[1 mark]*

11 P(Green or Orange) = 0.62 and P(Green) = 0.35, so
    P(Orange) = 0.62 − 0.35 = 0.27 *[1 mark]*
    P(Yellow) + P(not Yellow) = 1, so
    P(Yellow) = 1 − 0.92 = 0.08 *[1 mark]*
    P(Red) = 1 − (0.2 + 0.35 + 0.27 + 0.08) = 0.1 *[1 mark]*
    [3 marks available in total — as above]

12 a) 4 × 16 and 5 × 16 have a highest common factor of 16 and are in the ratio 4:5. 4 × 16 = 64, 5 × 16 = 80
        [2 marks available — 1 mark for each correct number]
    b) No — multiples of 64 and 80 are also in the ratio of 4:5 but their highest common factor would be more than 16, so there are no other possible pairs of numbers. *[1 mark]*

13 Angle $BEF = 46°$ (vertically opposite angles are equal)
    EBF is isosceles, so angle $BFE = (180° − 46°) ÷ 2 = 67°$
    Angle $p = 67°$ = angle BFE (alternate angles are equal)
    Angle $AGE = 67°$ = angle EBF (alternate angles are equal)
    Angle $ABE = 46°$ = angle BEF (alternate angles are equal)
    Angle $BAE = 46°$ = angle ABE (triangle ABE is isosceles)
    Angle $BAD = 67°$ = angle p (corresponding angles are equal)
    Angle $q = 67° − 46° = 21°$.
    [4 marks available — 1 mark for angle p, 1 mark for correct explanation, 1 mark for angle q, 1 mark for correct explanation]
    When there are lots of unknown angles in these questions it's a good idea to write angles you find on the diagram as you go.

14 a) Distance is given by the area under the graph.
        Split the graph into 5 sections and find the areas. E.g.

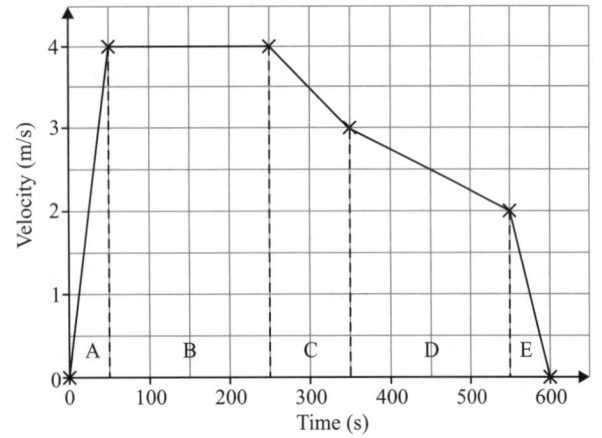

        $A = \frac{1}{2} × 50 × 4 = 100$ m, $B = 200 × 4 = 800$ m,
        $C = \frac{1}{2}(4 + 3) × 100 = 350$ m, $D = \frac{1}{2}(3 + 2) × 200 = 500$ m,
        $E = \frac{1}{2} × 50 × 2 = 50$ m
        Total distance = 100 + 800 + 350 + 500 + 50 = 1800 m
        [3 marks available — 1 mark for splitting the graph into sections, 1 mark for correctly calculating all areas, 1 mark for the correct answer]
    b) The gradient from (0, 0) to (600, 0) is 0, so the average acceleration is 0 m/s². *[1 mark]*

15 a) Rationalise the denominator by multiplying top and bottom by $\sqrt{5}$.
        $\frac{10}{\sqrt{5}} × \frac{\sqrt{5}}{\sqrt{5}} = \frac{10\sqrt{5}}{\sqrt{5}\sqrt{5}}$ *[1 mark]*
        $= \frac{10\sqrt{5}}{5} = 2\sqrt{5}$ *[1 mark]*
        $= \sqrt{4}\sqrt{5} = \sqrt{20}$ *[1 mark]*
        [3 marks available in total — as above]

b) Write the mixed numbers as improper fractions.
    $\left(1\frac{7}{9}\right)^{-1\frac{1}{2}} = \left(\frac{16}{9}\right)^{-\frac{3}{2}}$
    Turn the negative power into a positive one by inverting the fraction.
    $\left(\frac{16}{9}\right)^{-\frac{3}{2}} = \left(\frac{9}{16}\right)^{\frac{3}{2}}$ *[1 mark]*
    The power of $\frac{3}{2}$ is the same as taking the square root then cubing, so $\left(\frac{9}{16}\right)^{\frac{3}{2}} = \left(\sqrt{\frac{9}{16}}\right)^3 = \left(\frac{\sqrt{9}}{\sqrt{16}}\right)^3 = \left(\frac{3}{4}\right)^3$ *[1 mark]*
    $= \frac{27}{64}$ *[1 mark]*
    [3 marks available in total — as above]

16 1 m³ = 1 000 000 cm³ and 1 kg = 1000 g
    The density is $\frac{4000 \text{ kg}}{0.5 \text{ m}^3} = \frac{4\,000\,000 \text{ g}}{500\,000 \text{ cm}^3}$ *[1 mark]*
    $= \frac{40}{5} = 8$ g/cm³ which is the same density as iron. *[1 mark]*
    [2 marks available in total — as above]

17 The sale price of the shorts is 90% of the original price.
    90% = £18.00
    10% = £18.00 ÷ 9 = £2.00
    100% = £2.00 × 10 = £20 *[1 mark]*
    1 part is £20 ÷ 5 = £4, so the original price of the jeans is £4 × 7 = £28 *[1 mark]*
    10% of £28 = £28 ÷ 10 = £2.80
    20% of £28 = £2.80 × 2 = £5.60 *[1 mark]*
    So the sale price of the jeans is £28 − £5.60 = £22.40 *[1 mark]*
    [4 marks available in total — as above]

18 Multiply two brackets out first and then multiply the product by the third bracket.
    $(x + 3)(x + 5) = x^2 + 5x + 3x + 15 = x^2 + 8x + 15$
    $(x^2 + 8x + 15)(x − 2) = x^3 − 2x^2 + 8x^2 − 16x + 15x − 30$
    $= x^3 + 6x^2 − x − 30$
    [3 marks available — 1 mark for multiplying 2 brackets correctly, 1 mark for multiplying 3 brackets correctly, 1 mark for the correct answer]

19 a) Length $BC = 2 − (−4) = 6$
        $AC = BC = 6$ as ABC is isosceles. *[1 mark]*
        ACD is a right-angled triangle, so
        $\tan 60° = \frac{6}{CD}$ *[1 mark]*
        $\sqrt{3} = \frac{6}{CD}$, so $CD = \frac{6}{\sqrt{3}}$ *[1 mark]*
        $CD = \frac{6}{\sqrt{3}} × \frac{\sqrt{3}}{\sqrt{3}} = \frac{6\sqrt{3}}{3} = 2\sqrt{3}$ *[1 mark]*
        [4 marks available in total — as above]
    b) Find AD using Pythagoras' theorem.
        $AD^2 = 6^2 + (2\sqrt{3})^2$
        $AD^2 = 36 + (4 × \sqrt{3}\sqrt{3}) = 36 + 12 = 48$
        $AD = \sqrt{48} = 4\sqrt{3}$
        [2 marks available — 1 mark for using Pythagoras' theorem, 1 mark for the correct answer]
        You could also use trigonometry with sin 60° or cos 60°.

20 The ratio of the pressures is 3:5 so the pressure on face A is $\frac{3}{5}$ of the pressure when on face B. *[1 mark]*
    Pressure $= \frac{\text{force}}{\text{area}}$, so force = pressure × area
    The force is the same, whichever face the prism is on, so if the pressure exerted on face A is $\frac{3}{5}$ as much as on face B, then the area of A must be $\frac{5}{3}$ times bigger.
    Area of face B $= \frac{1}{2} × 8 × 3 = 12$ cm² *[1 mark]*
    Area of face A $= \frac{5}{3} × 12 = 20$ cm² *[1 mark]*
    $l = \frac{20}{5} = 4$ cm *[1 mark]*
    [4 marks available in total — as above]

Answers

These answers and mark schemes will show you exactly how to do each question and where you get the marks. If you've got to the correct answer by a different method, you can still award yourself full marks, as long as your answer and working are absolutely clear...

Set 1 Paper 1 — Non-calculator

1. a) $3\mathbf{a} = 3 \times \begin{pmatrix} 8 \\ 3 \end{pmatrix} = \begin{pmatrix} 24 \\ 9 \end{pmatrix}$ *[1 mark]*

   b) $\mathbf{a} - 4\mathbf{b} = \begin{pmatrix} 8 \\ 3 \end{pmatrix} - 4\begin{pmatrix} 1 \\ -7 \end{pmatrix} = \begin{pmatrix} 8 \\ 3 \end{pmatrix} - \begin{pmatrix} 4 \\ -28 \end{pmatrix}$ *[1 mark]*

   $= \begin{pmatrix} 4 \\ 31 \end{pmatrix}$ *[1 mark]*

   [2 marks available in total — as above]

2. 140% of $x = 28$,
   10% of $x = 28 \div 14 = 2$ *[1 mark]*
   $x = 2 \times 10 = 20$ *[1 mark]*
   [2 marks available in total — as above]

3. Side Elevation: *[1 mark]*

   Plan View: *[1 mark]*

   [2 marks available in total — as above]

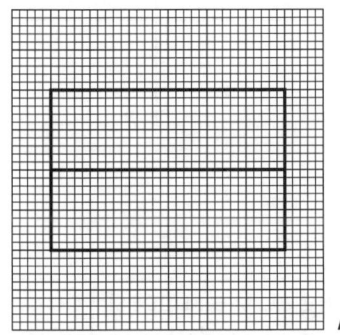

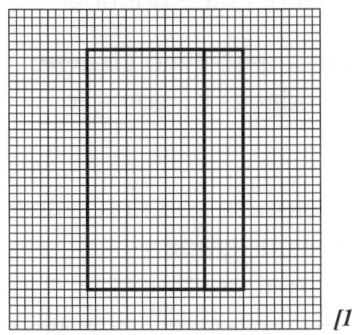

4. a) $x = 3y - 5$
   $x + 5 = 3y$ *[1 mark]*
   $y = \dfrac{x+5}{3}$ *[1 mark]*
   [2 marks available in total — as above]

   b) Take out a common factor of $4x$.
   $8x^2 - 12xy = 4x(2x - 3y)$
   [2 marks available — 2 marks for the correct answer, otherwise 1 mark for taking out a common factor of 4 or x correctly]

5. a) P = {2, 3, 5, 7, 11, 13, 17, 19} and Q = {1, 2, 3, 4, 6, 8, 12}
   P ∩ Q is the set of numbers that appear in both sets = {2, 3}
   [2 marks available — 2 marks if both elements are correct, otherwise 1 mark if one element is omitted or if an extra element is included]

   b) n(P ∪ Q) is the number of members in the set P ∪ Q
   P ∪ Q = {1, 2, 3, 4, 5, 6, 7, 8, 11, 12, 13, 17, 19} *[1 mark]*
   n(P ∪ Q) = 13 *[1 mark]*
   [2 marks available in total — as above]

6. E.g. No — to confirm her statement she would need to ask everyone in the school, as it only takes one person to choose history to make her claim false.
   [1 mark for a suitable explanation]

7. a) *[1 mark for plotting both points correctly]*

   b) Draw a line of best fit and read up to the time at 7.5 km. 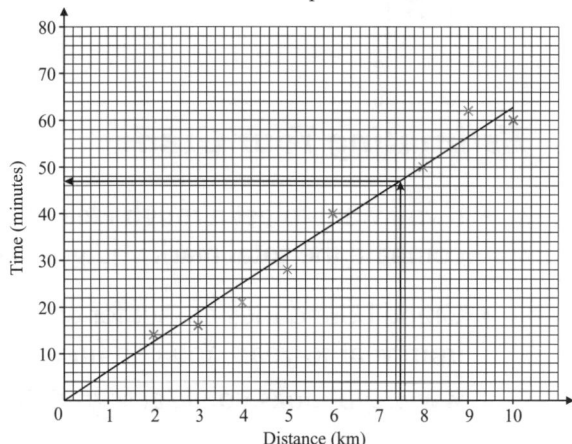

   47 minutes
   [2 marks available — 1 mark for a suitable line of best fit, 1 mark for an answer in the range of 45-49 minutes]

   c) E.g. When he runs a greater distance his speed is likely to decrease, so it will take longer per km.
   [1 mark for a suitable explanation]

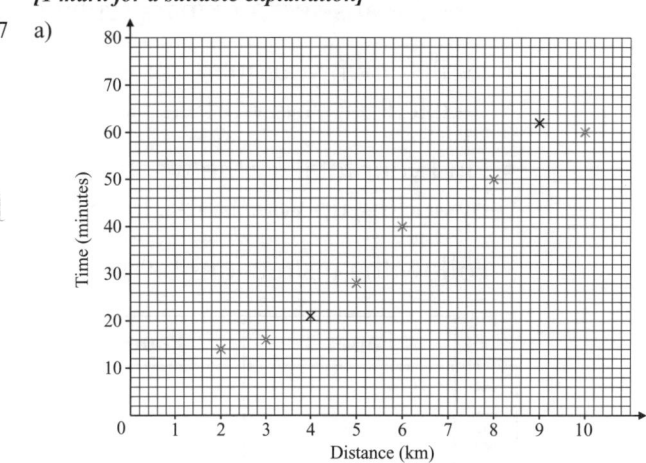

8. Find how many tins are eaten each day then divide 24 by that answer. Put fractions over a common denominator:
   $\dfrac{2}{3} + \dfrac{2}{5} = \dfrac{10}{15} + \dfrac{6}{15} = \dfrac{16}{15}$ *[1 mark]*
   $24 \div \dfrac{16}{15} = 24 \times \dfrac{15}{16}$ *[1 mark]* $= 3 \times \dfrac{15}{2} = \dfrac{45}{2} = 22.5$,
   which is 22 whole days. *[1 mark]*
   [3 marks available in total — as above]

9. a) Round each number to 1 s.f. and replace in the calculation.
   $\dfrac{200 \times 0.07}{0.7} = 200 \times \dfrac{0.07}{0.7} = 200 \times 0.1 = 20$
   [2 marks available — 1 mark for correctly rounding all numbers, 1 mark for the correct answer]

   b) The numbers in the numerator were both rounded down which makes the estimate smaller. The number in the denominator was rounded up which also makes the estimate smaller. So, the estimate is an underestimate.
   [1 mark for a correct explanation]

Marking Your Papers

- Do a complete exam (paper 1, paper 2 and paper 3).
- Use the answers and mark scheme in this booklet to mark each exam paper.
- Write down your mark for each paper in the table below — each paper is worth a maximum of 80 marks.
- Find your total for the whole exam (out of a maximum of 240 marks) by adding up your marks from all three papers.
- Follow the instructions below to estimate your grade.

	Paper 1	Paper 2	Paper 3	Total	Grade
SET 1	34	34	34	100	4
SET 2					

Estimating Your Grade

250   6   5   4
115 90 65 H
125 100 F

- If you want to get a **rough idea** of the grade you're working at, we suggest you compare the **total mark** you got in **each set** to the latest set of grade boundaries.
- Grade boundaries are set for each individual exam, so they're likely to **change** from year to year. You can find the latest set of grade boundaries by going to **www.cgpbooks.co.uk/gcsegradeboundaries**
- Jot down the marks required for each grade in the table below so you don't have to refer back to the website. Use these marks to **estimate your grade**.
  If you're borderline, don't push yourself up a grade — the real examiners won't.

Total mark required for each grade						
Grade	9	8	7	6	5	4
Total mark out of 240				STRONG	STRONG	GRADE STD

- Remember, this will only be a **rough guide**, and grade boundaries will be different for different exams, but it should help you to see how you're getting on.

Published by CGP

Contributors: Mark Moody and Kieran Wardell.

Editors: Liam Dyer, Rob Harrison and Shaun Harrogate.

Many thanks to Simon Little and Rosie Hanson for the proofreading.

www.cgpbooks.co.uk
Clipart from Corel®
Printed by Elanders Ltd, Newcastle upon Tyne.

Text, design, layout and original illustrations
© Coordination Group Publications Ltd. (CGP) 2016
All rights reserved.

Photocopying more than 5% of a paper is not permitted, even if you have a CLA licence.
Extra copies are available from CGP with next day delivery • 0800 1712 712 • www.cgpbooks.co.uk

22 At a party, there are c children and a adults.
The ratio of the number of children to the number of adults at the party is $c:a$.
3 more children and 3 more adults arrive and the ratio is now $2:3$.
Then 2 children leave and 2 more adults arrive, and the ratio becomes $1:2$.

Find the ratio $c:a$ in its lowest terms.

....
[Total 6 marks]

[TOTAL FOR PAPER = 80 MARKS]

21 A circle, with centre O, has a tangent at A that passes through point D.
BCD is a straight line.

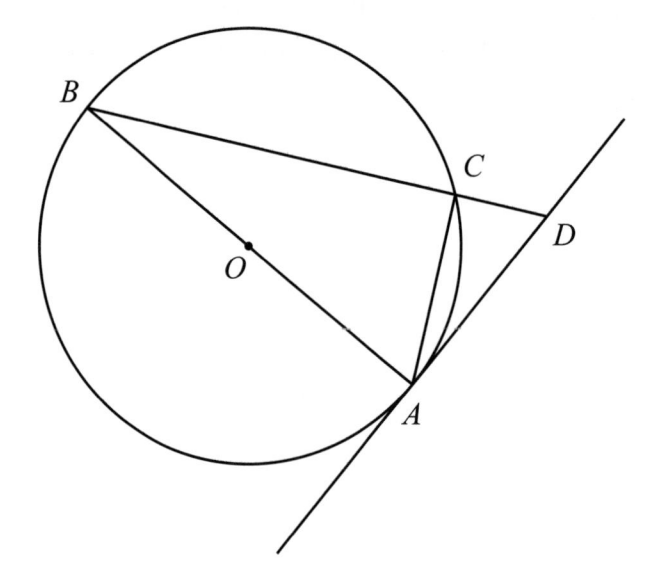

Show that ABC, ABD and ACD are all similar triangles.

[Total 4 marks]

19 Show that $2\sin 60° \times \tan 30° = 1$

[Total 3 marks]

20 (a) Write the expression $x^2 - 6x - 2$ in the form $(x + a)^2 + b$

....
[2]

(b) Write down the coordinates of the turning point of the graph $y = x^2 - 6x - 2$

....
[1]

[Total 3 marks]

18 The diagram shows a sketch of the graph $y = f(x)$. The graph passes through the points $(-2, 0)$, $(2, 0)$ and $(0, -3)$. Sketch the graphs for the following functions, showing clearly the points where the graphs cross the x-axis and y-axis.

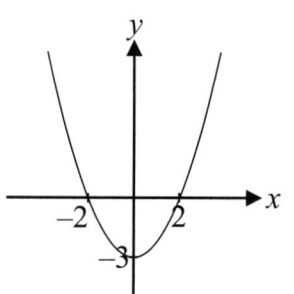

(a) $y = f(x + 2)$

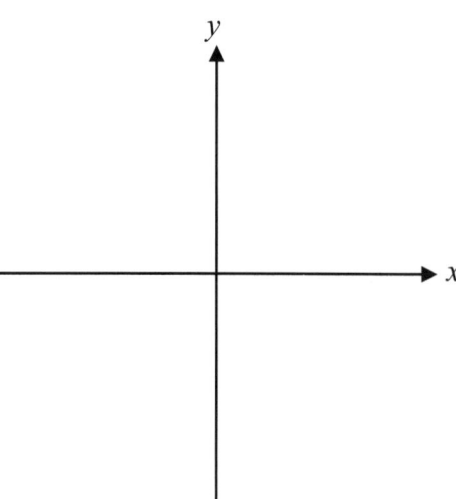

[2]

(b) $y = -f(x)$

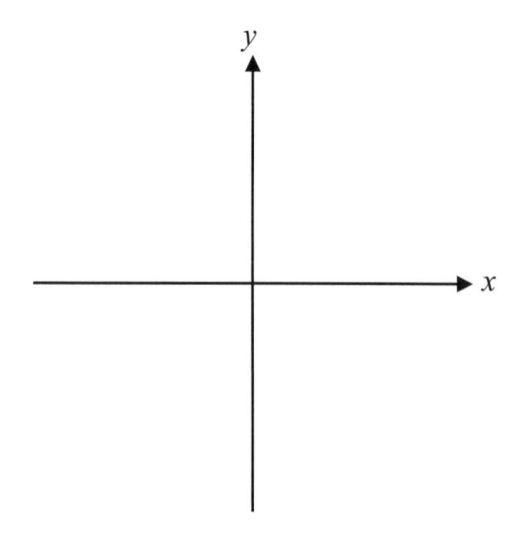

[2]

[Total 4 marks]

17 The shape below is a sector of a circle.

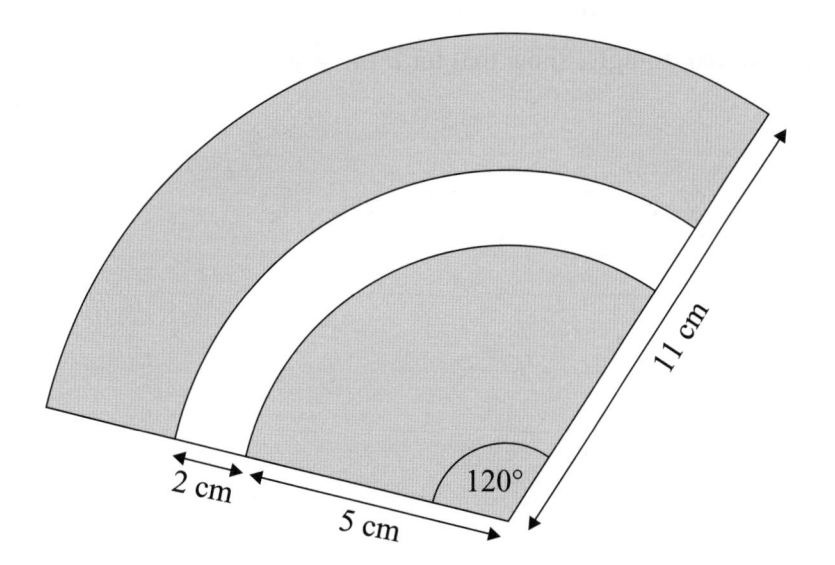

Calculate the shaded area of the shape. Give your answer in terms of π.

.... cm^2

[Total 4 marks]

16 a is an acute angle such that $\sin a = \dfrac{3}{2\sqrt{6}}$

(a) By sketching a right angled triangle, show that $\tan a = \dfrac{3}{\sqrt{15}}$

[3]

(b) On the axes below, sketch the graph of $y = \sin x$ for $0° \leq x \leq 360°$.

[2]

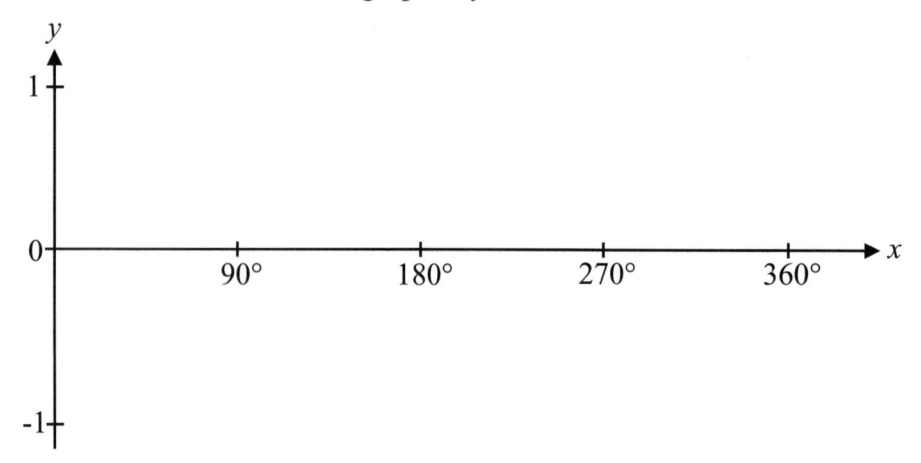

(c) $\sin^{-1}\left(\dfrac{1}{2}\right) = 30°$

Solve the equation $\sin x = -\dfrac{1}{2}$ for $0° \leq x \leq 360°$.

....
[2]

[Total 7 marks]

14 Calculate $(3.2 \times 10^4) \div (8 \times 10^{-2})$
Give your answer in standard form.

....
[Total 2 marks]

15 On the grid below, shade the region that satisfies the following inequalities:

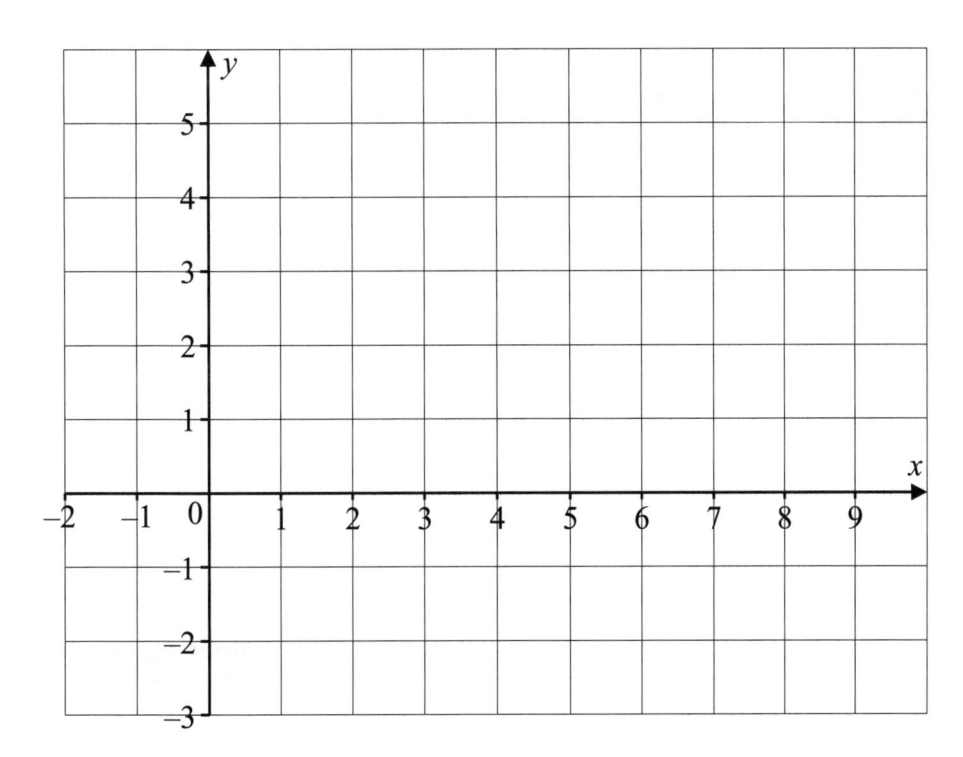

$2y + x \leq 8$ $x \geq 1$ $y \geq x - 1$

[Total 4 marks]

13 (a) Enlarge shape T by a scale factor −1 , with centre of enlargement (−1, 1). Label the enlarged shape S.

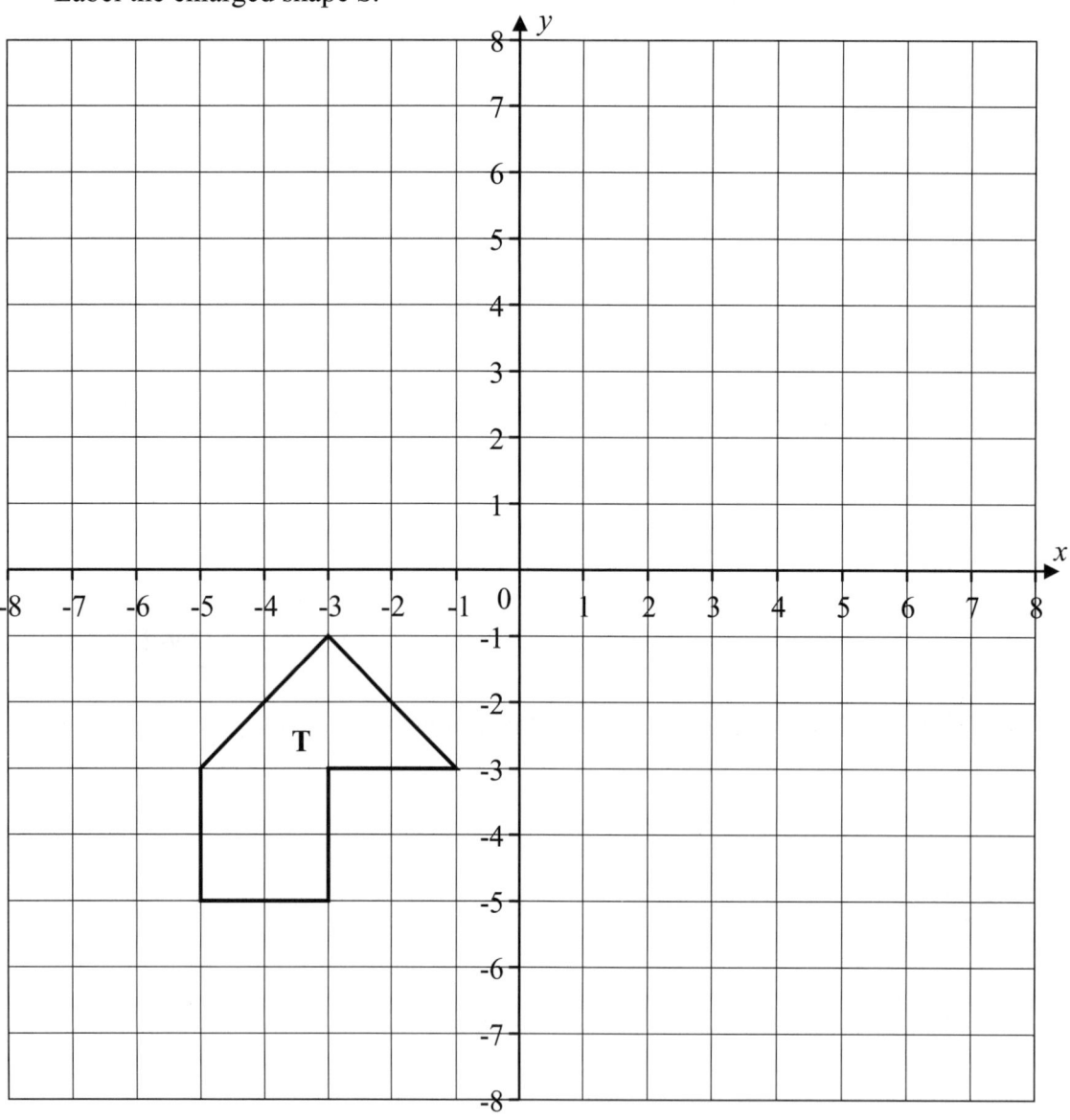

[2]

(b) Describe another transformation that maps Shape T onto Shape S.

....

....

[2]

[Total 4 marks]

11 Make x the subject of $2y = \dfrac{3x}{2-5x}$

....

[Total 3 marks]

12 Jen records the number of miles she travels by tram each day.
After 6 days, her mean distance is 5.5 miles.

After 7 days, her mean distance had increased to 6 miles.
How many miles did Jen travel by tram on the 7th day?

.... miles

[Total 3 marks]

9 Use the approximation 5 miles ≈ 8 km to show that a car moving at a speed of 45 mph is travelling approximately 20 m/s.

[Total 3 marks]

10 Scott is a bricklayer. In his latest building project, it took 5400 bricks to build a bungalow. He was able to lay roughly 3000 bricks every 5 days.

(a) How many days would it take for a team of 3 bricklayers to lay the bricks required for 20 bungalows?

.... days
[3]

(b) State two assumptions that you have made in part (a).

1) ....

....

2) ....

....
[2]

[Total 5 marks]

7 A fair 6-sided dice and a fair 10-sided dice are rolled repeatedly over the course of a game.

The 6-sided dice (numbered 1-6) is rolled 300 times.
The 10-sided dice (numbered 1-10) is rolled 200 times.

Calculate an estimate for the number of times a prime number is rolled.

....
[Total 3 marks]

8 Mesut is investigating the average age of people who use his local sports centre.
On a Monday morning, he asked people at the sports centre their ages.
His results are shown in the table:

Age	12 –18	19 – 30	31 – 50	Over 50
Frequency	10	24	12	14

Mesut says, "5 in 6 users of the sports centre are over 18. This shows that the sports centre should do more to encourage children and teenagers to use the sports centre."

Give reasons why Mesut's conclusion might not be correct.

....

....

....

....

....

[Total 2 marks]

6 Written as a product of powers of its prime factors, $126 = 2 \times 3^2 \times 7$.

(a) Write 392 as a product of powers of its prime factors.

....
[3]

(b) Find the highest common factor of 392 and 126.

....
[1]

k is the smallest integer that can be multiplied by 126 to give a square number.

(c) Find the value of k.

$k =$ ....
[1]

[Total 5 marks]

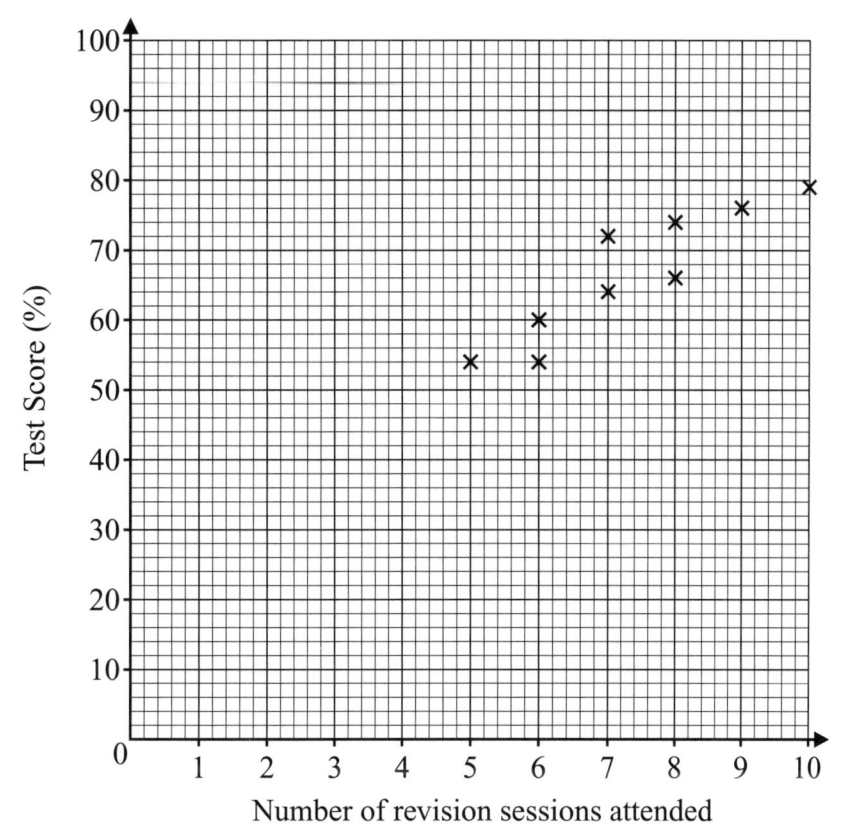

5 A teacher recorded the number of revision sessions attended by some students and the mark they scored in a test. The results are shown in this scatter diagram.

(a) Draw a line of best fit.

[1]

(b) Describe the relationship between the number of revision sessions attended and the test score achieved by the students.

....

....

[1]

(c) Katherine was absent for the test. The teacher says, "Katherine attended two revision sessions, so she would have scored about 30% in the test."

Comment on the reliability of the teacher's statement.

....

....

....

....

[2]

[Total 4 marks]

3 (a) Find 96 as a percentage of 75.

.... %
[2]

(b) Increase 60 by 12%.

....
[2]

[Total 4 marks]

4 A squad of 14 players is selected for a mixed football tournament.
The rules state that the ratio of boys to girls per squad must be no greater than 3 : 2

What is the maximum number of boys that can be selected for the squad?

....

[Total 2 marks]

Answer ALL the questions.

Write your answers in the spaces provided.

You must show all of your working.

1   Work out $85.6 \div 0.4$

....

[Total 2 marks]

2   Work out $3\frac{1}{4} \times 1\frac{3}{5}$. Give your answer as a mixed number.

....

[Total 3 marks]

General Certificate of Secondary Education

GCSE
Mathematics (Grade 9-1)
Higher Tier

Practice Set 2
Paper 1: Non-calculator

Time allowed: 1 hour 30 minutes

Centre name				
Centre number				
Candidate number				

Surname
Other names
Candidate signature

In addition to this paper you should have:
- A pen, pencil and eraser.
- A ruler.
- A protractor.
- A pair of compasses.

Calculators may **not** be used.

Instructions to candidates
- Write your name and other details in the spaces provided above.
- Answer all questions in the spaces provided.
- In calculations show clearly how you worked out your answers.
- Diagrams are **not** drawn accurately unless otherwise indicated.

Information for candidates
- There are 80 marks available for this paper.
- The marks available are given in brackets at the end of each question.
- You may get marks for method, even if your answer is incorrect.

Advice to candidates
- Work steadily through the paper.
- Don't spend too long on one question.
- If you have time at the end, go back and check your answers.

For examiner's use

Q	Mark	Q	Mark
1		12	
2		13	
3		14	
4		15	
5		16	
6		17	
7		18	
8		19	
9		20	
10		21	
11		22	
Total			

Exam Set MHB45 / MXHP43

© CGP 2016 — copying more than 5% of this paper is not permitted

21 The diagram shows a shaded circle drawn inside a sector of a larger circle, with centre O.

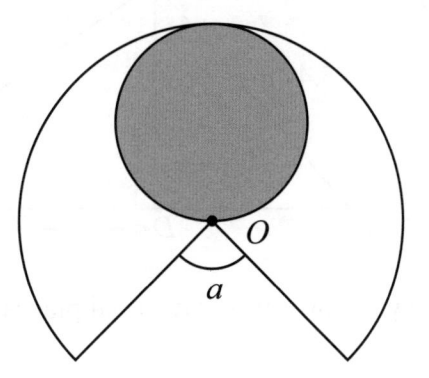

If 30% of the sector is covered by the shaded circle, find the angle a.

$a = $ .... °

[Total 4 marks]

[TOTAL FOR PAPER = 80 MARKS]

19 The diagram shows triangle *ABC* split into two right-angled triangles.
Angle *ABC* is 34°.
DB = 6 cm, *AC* = 5.4 cm

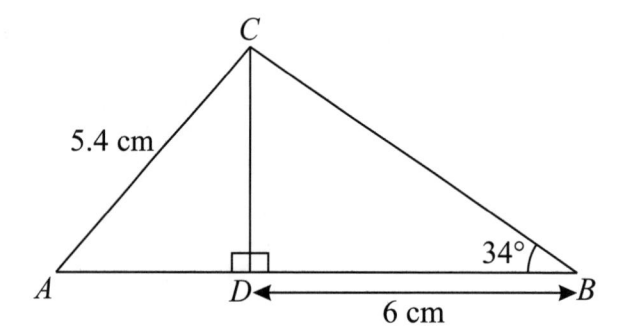

Find the area of triangle *ABC*. Give your answer to 2 decimal places.

.... cm²

[Total 4 marks]

20 Prove that $(3n + 2)^2 - 1$ is a multiple of 3 for all positive integer values of *n*.

[Total 3 marks]

17 Show that the lowest common multiple of 450^3 and 240^3 is 60^6.

[Total 4 marks]

18 Simplify $\dfrac{6x-3}{2x^2+7x-4} \div \dfrac{15}{x^2-16}$

....
[Total 4 marks]

16 Katie's speed was measured as she skated for 12 seconds.
The graph shows the speed in metres per second, t seconds after she started skating.

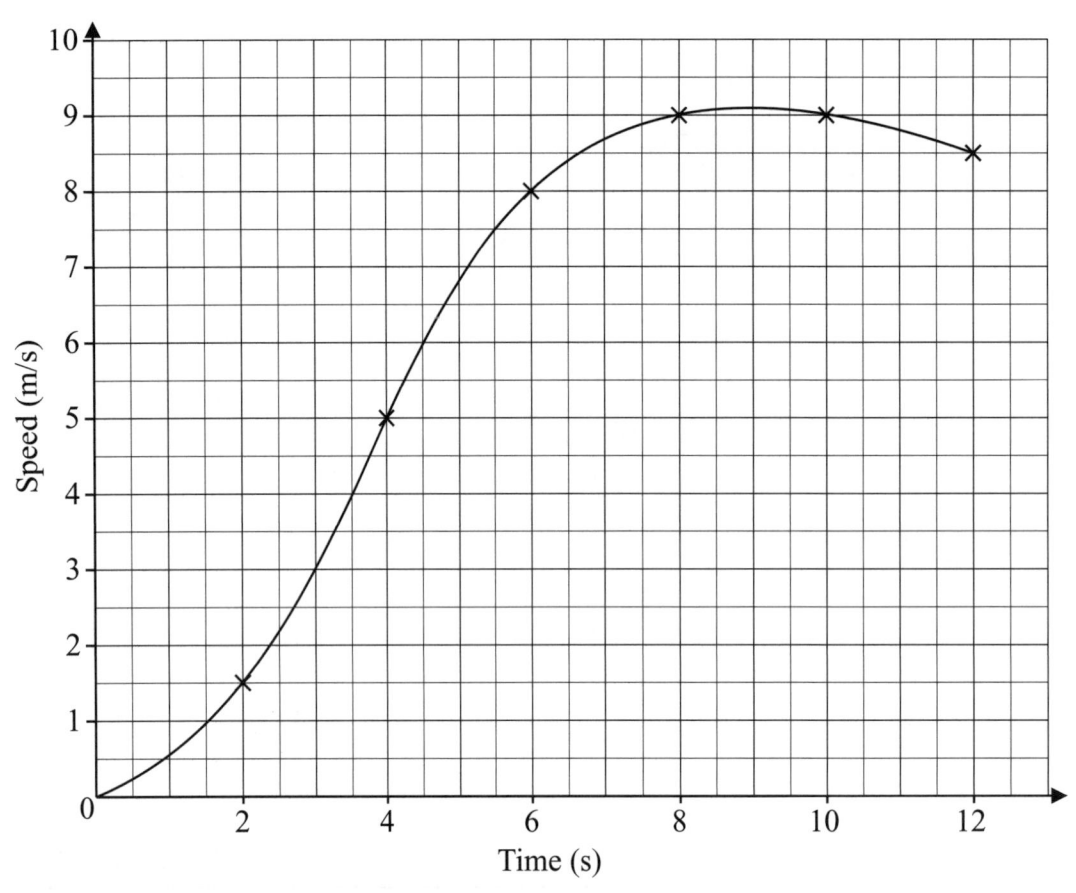

(a) Calculate an estimate for Katie's acceleration when $t = 6$.

.... m/s²
[2]

(b) Draw 3 strips of equal width on the graph to work out an estimate for the total distance Katie skates in the first 12 seconds.

.... m
[3]
[Total 5 marks]

15 The number of people living in a town increased by 7% between 2010 and 2015.
In 2015, the number of people in the town was 32 000 to the nearest 1000.

(a) Estimate how many more people live in the town now compared to 5 years ago.

....
[2]

(b) Mikko says "As 32 000 is rounded to the nearest 1000, the estimate to part (a) could be as much as 500 away from the actual answer."

Is Mikko correct? Show calculations to support your answer.

....

....

....

....

....

....

[3]

[Total 5 marks]

13 Show that the straight line through the points (2, 7) and (5, 13) is perpendicular to the line $2y = 13 - x$

[Total 3 marks]

14 Aaron invests £750 in a bank account that pays a fixed rate of compound interest each year. After 4 years, he has a total of £844.13 in the account.

What is the annual rate of interest?

.... %

[Total 3 marks]

12 Eleven science students sat a chemistry exam.
The number of marks scored by the students are shown below.

   8   9   11   11   12   15   16   17   19   23   24

(a) Draw a box plot to show this information.

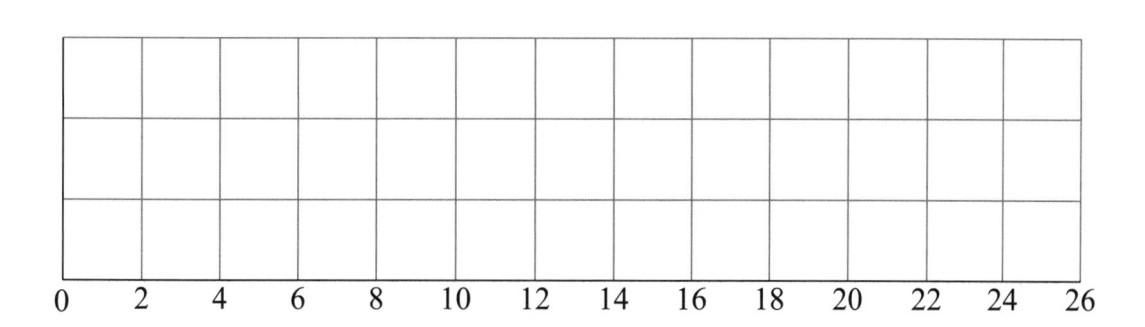

[3]

The same students also sat a physics exam.
The box plot below shows a summary of their scores.

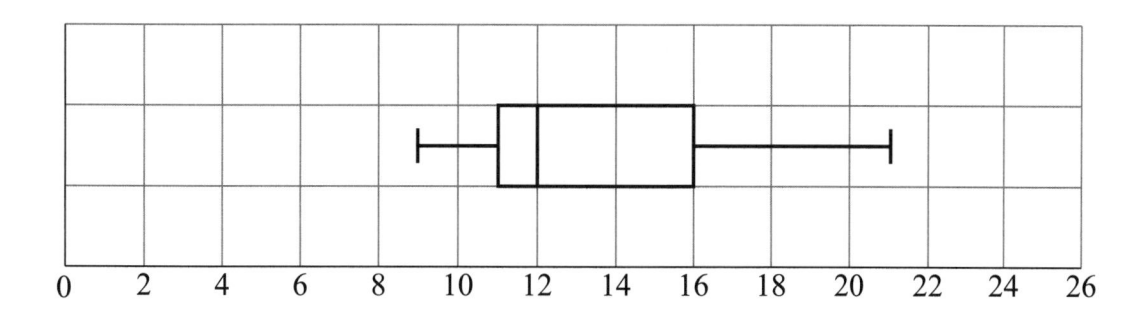

(b) Compare the marks the students scored in the chemistry and physics exams.

....

....

....

....

[2]

[Total 5 marks]

11 The formula for the period, T seconds, of a pendulum of length l metres is given by:
$$T = 2\pi\sqrt{\frac{l}{g}}$$

At the equator, $g = 9.78$ m/s^2.

(a) Find the period of a pendulum, of length 30 cm, at the Equator.
Give your answer to 3 significant figures.

$T = $ .... seconds
[2]

At the North Pole, $g = 9.832$ m/s^2.

(b) The period of a 30 cm pendulum is measured at the Equator, then at the North Pole. What is the percentage change in the period of the pendulum from the Equator to the North Pole. Give your answer to 3 significant figures.

.... %
[3]

[Total 5 marks]

9 An insurance company analyses the impact of its TV adverts.
They find that each week, the number of new customers (c) is directly proportional to the square of the number of TV adverts placed (a).

One week, 10 TV adverts were placed and the company got 1500 new customers.

Find how many TV adverts had been placed in a week when the company got 2940 new customers.

....

[Total 3 marks]

10 The diagram shows two identical regular pentagons, each with a side on the line AB.

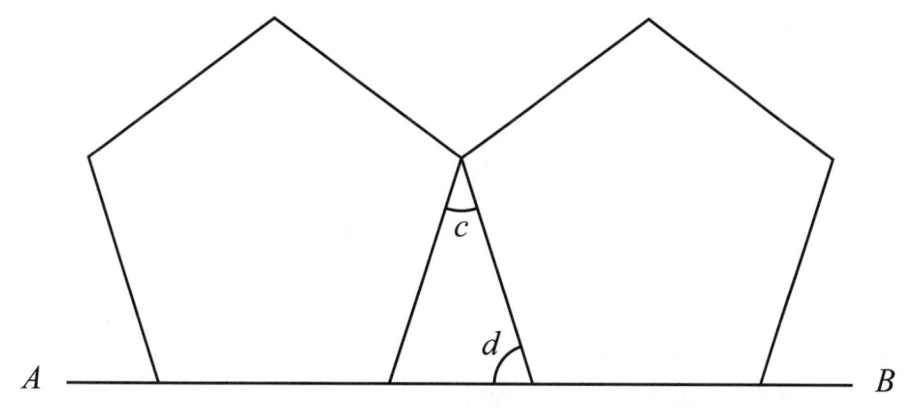

Show that the sizes of the angles c and d are in the ratio $1:2$.

[Total 3 marks]

8 There are 30 students in a maths class. 60% of the students attended a revision class and 15 of the attendees achieved their target grade

Altogether, $\frac{2}{3}$ of the students achieved their target grade.

(a) Complete the frequency tree to show this information.

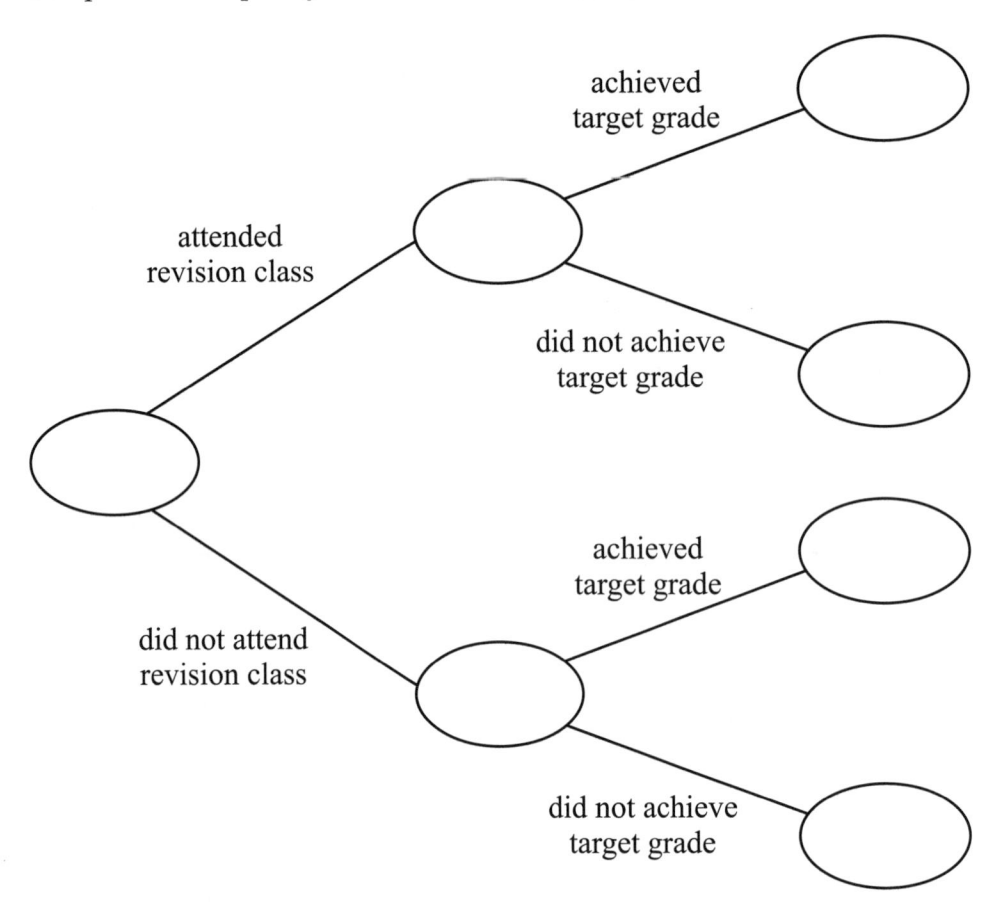

[3]

(b) What is the probability that a randomly chosen student achieved their target grade given that they did not attend a revision class?

....
[1]

[Total 4 marks]

7   For all values of x

$$f(x) = 3x - 5$$
$$g(x) = x^2 - 3$$

(a) Find the value of g(–2)

....
[1]

(b) Find $f^{-1}(x)$

$f^{-1}(x) = $ ....
[2]

(c) Show that $gf(x) = 9x^2 - 30x + 22$

[2]

[Total 5 marks]

6 The sets ξ, M and F are shown below.

ξ = {1, 2, 3, 4, 5, 6, 7, 8, 9, 10, 11, 12}
M = {multiples of 3}
F = {factors of 60}

(a) Complete the Venn diagram.

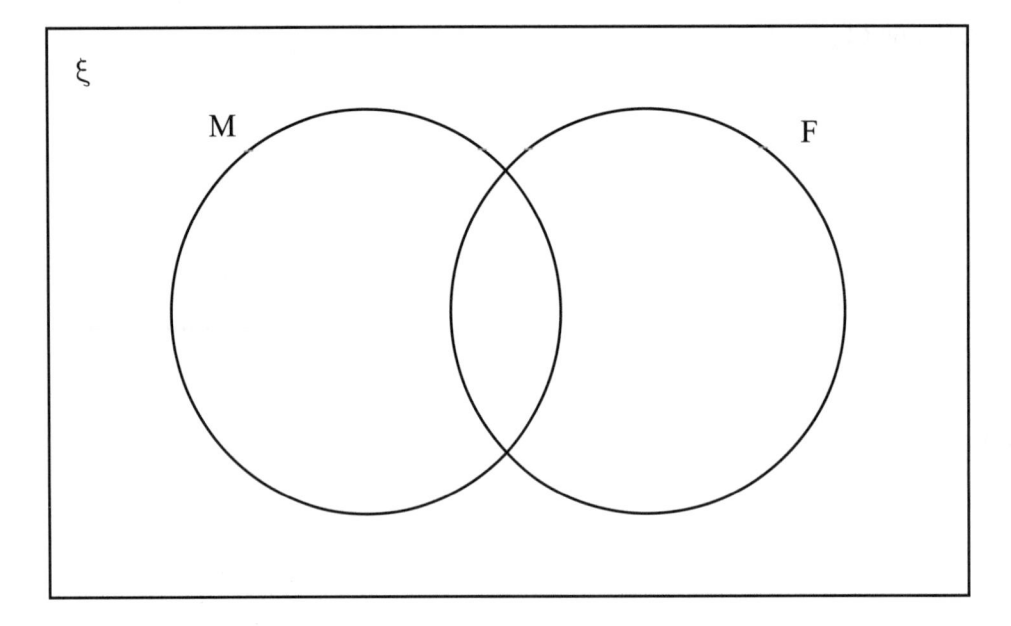

[3]

One of the numbers is chosen at random.

(b) Show that the probabilities of the number being in set (M ∩ F) or set (M ∪ F)' are equal.

[2]

[Total 5 marks]

4 A box contains 123 chocolates, which are either plain, milk or white chocolate.

The ratio of plain to milk chocolates is 2 : 3
The ratio of milk to white chocolates is 7 : 2

Find the number of plain chocolates in the box.

....
[Total 3 marks]

5 The first four terms of an arithmetic sequence are:

$$3 \quad 10 \quad 17 \quad 24$$

(a) Write an expression for the nth term of this sequence.

....
[2]

(b) Show that 1024 is not a term of this sequence.

[2]
[Total 4 marks]

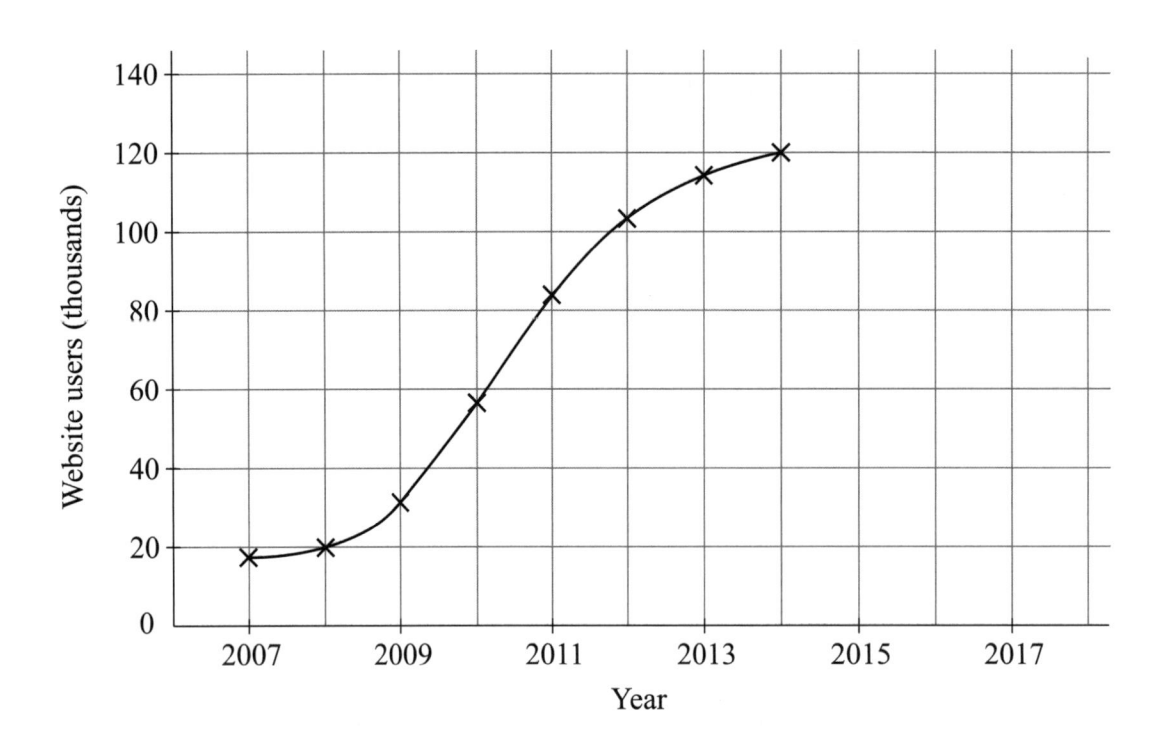

3 The time series graph shows the number of users of a social media website between 2007 and 2014.

(a) Describe the growth rate in the number of website users between 2007 and 2014.

....

....

....

....
[2]

(b) Use the graph to predict the number of users of the website in 2017. Comment on the reliability of your answer.

....

....

....

....
[2]

[Total 4 marks]

Answer ALL the questions.

Write your answers in the spaces provided.

You must show all of your working.

1 A café offers a meal deal for £3.50, consisting of a sandwich, a packet of crisps and a drink.

   7 different sandwiches, 4 different flavours of crisps and 5 different drinks are available in the meal deal.

   A customer claims to have tried every possible meal deal combination exactly once. How much has this customer spent on meal deals in total?

   £ ....

   [Total 2 marks]

2 A fathom is an old unit of length, typically used to measure the depth of water. Given that 1 fathom ≈ 1.8 metres, work out the number of fathoms in 1.782 km.

   .... fathoms

   [Total 2 marks]

CGP Practice Exam Paper
GCSE Mathematics

General Certificate of Secondary Education

GCSE
Mathematics (Grade 9-1)
Higher Tier

Centre name

Centre number

Candidate number

Practice Set 2
Paper 2: Calculator

Surname

Other names

Candidate signature

Time allowed: 1 hour 30 minutes

In addition to this paper you should have:
- A pen, pencil and eraser.
- A ruler.
- A protractor.
- A pair of compasses.
- A calculator.

Instructions to candidates
- Write your name and other details in the spaces provided above.
- Answer all questions in the spaces provided.
- In calculations show clearly how you worked out your answers.
- Diagrams are **not** drawn accurately unless otherwise indicated.
- Calculators may be used — if your calculator doesn't have a π button, take the value of π to be 3.142

Information for candidates
- There are 80 marks available for this paper.
- The marks available are given in brackets at the end of each question.
- You may get marks for method, even if your answer is incorrect.

Advice to candidates
- Work steadily through the paper.
- Don't spend too long on one question.
- If you have time at the end, go back and check your answers.

For examiner's use
Q	Mark	Q	Mark
1		12	
2		13	
3		14	
4		15	
5		16	
6		17	
7		18	
8		19	
9		20	
10		21	
11			
Total			

Exam Set MHB45 / MXHP43

© CGP 2016 — copying more than 5% of this paper is not permitted

21 The diagram shows the parallelogram *OABC*.
The point *D* lies on *AC*, such that *AD*:*DC* = 3:2.
The point *E* lies $\frac{2}{3}$ of the way along line *CB*.

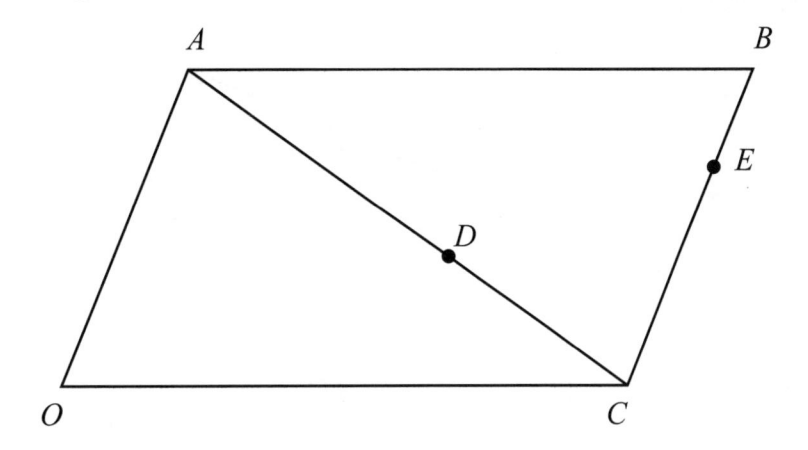

$\overrightarrow{OA}$ = **a** and $\overrightarrow{OC}$ = **c**
Show that *ODE* is a straight line.

[Total 5 marks]

[TOTAL FOR PAPER = 80 MARKS]

20 The points *A*, *B* and *C* lie on a circle.
Point *O* lies at the centre of the circle.
Lines *DF* and *DE* are tangents to the circle at points *A* and *C* respectively.
Lines *AB* and *DE* are parallel.
Angle *BCE* = *n*

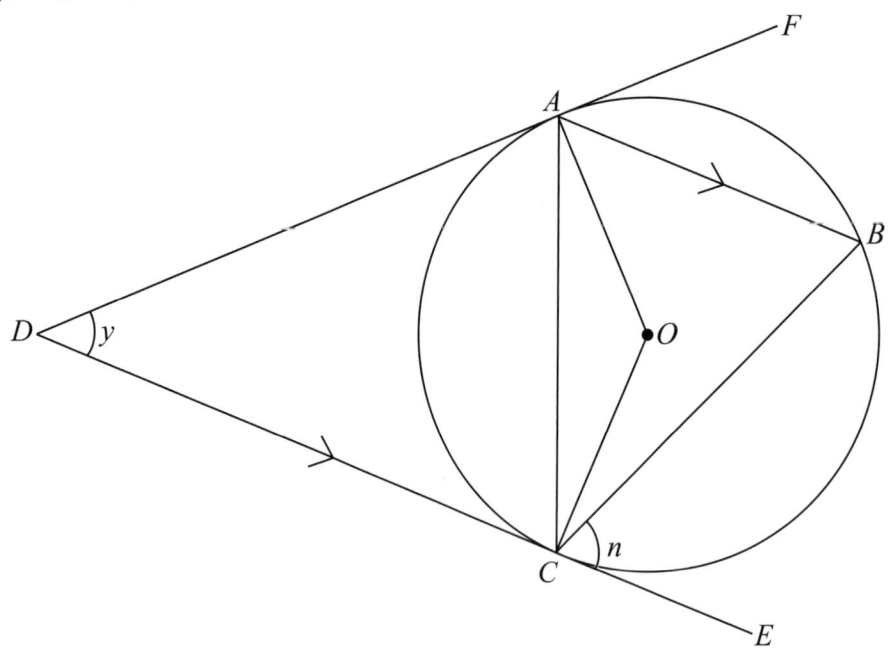

Show that $y = 180° - 2n$. You must give a reason for each stage of your working.

[Total 4 marks]

19 The functions f and g are defined as follows.

$$f(x) = 2x + 3$$
$$g(x) = f^{-1}(x)$$

(a) Solve the equation $f(x)^2 = 5$. Give your answers to 2 decimal places.

x = ... or x = ...
[3]

(b) Work out the value of $gg(x)$ when $f(x) = 27$

....
[3]

[Total 6 marks]

18 The diagram below shows two triangles, *ACB* and *ACD*.

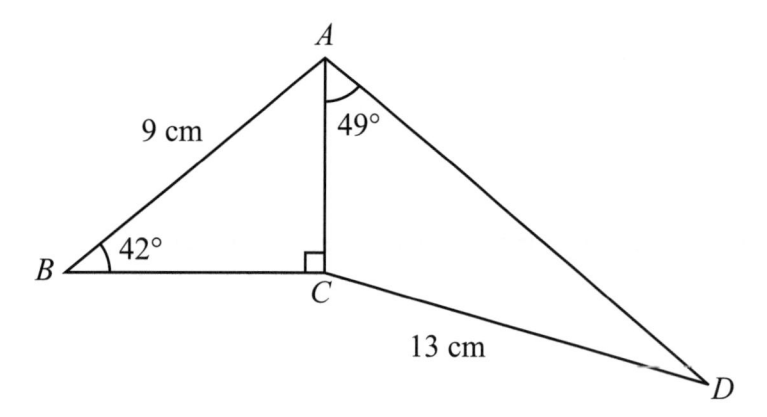

Find the size of angle *ADC*.

angle *ADC* = ...°

[Total 4 marks]

16 y is inversely proportional to the square root of x.
When $y = 12$, $x = 0.09$

Find the value of x when $y = 9$

$x = $ ....

[Total 3 marks]

17 The volumes of two spheres are in the ratio $1:8$.
The surface area of the larger sphere is 28 cm².

Surface area of a sphere $= 4\pi r^2$

What is the radius, r, of the smaller sphere?
Give your answer to 2 decimal places.

$r = $ .... cm

[Total 4 marks]

15 The incomplete Venn diagram shows how many Year 11 students study Spanish, French and German. There are 50 Year 11 students in total.

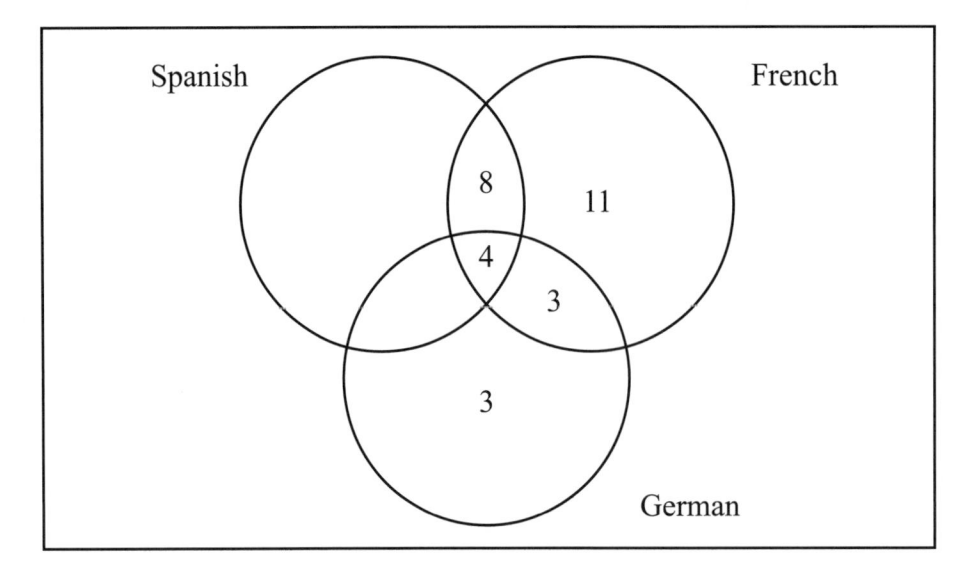

(a) 27 students study Spanish. 6 students study Spanish and German.
Use this information to complete the Venn diagram.

[2]

(b) If a student is chosen at random, what is the probability that they study exactly one language?

....
[2]

(c) If a student studying French is chosen at random, what is the probability that they study exactly one other language?

....
[2]

[Total 6 marks]

14 (a) Write an expression for the nth term of the following sequence.

    8   13   18   23   28   ...

[2]

(b) Use your answer from part (a) to write an expression for the nth term of the following sequence.

    13   33   63   103   153   ...

[3]

(c) Are all the numbers of the second sequence also in the first sequence? Explain your answer.

[1]

[Total 6 marks]

12 Tanya and Stuart are taking part in a charity bike race.
They have 9 hours to complete the 190 km course.
They rode 141 km in the first $6\frac{3}{4}$ hours.

Do you think they will finish the course within the target time? Explain your answer.

....

....

....

....

....

....

....

[Total 2 marks]

13 Show that $\dfrac{4}{3+\sqrt{5}} + \sqrt{5} = 3$

[Total 3 marks]

11 Prove that the sum of the squares of any two consecutive odd numbers is 2 more than a multiple of 8.

[Total 4 marks]

10 The table shows the distribution of marks in a School Maths challenge.

Mark (*m*)	$m \leq 40$	$m \leq 60$	$m \leq 80$	$m \leq 100$	$m \leq 120$
Cumulative Frequency	6	20	50	68	80

(a) Draw a cumulative frequency graph to show these results.

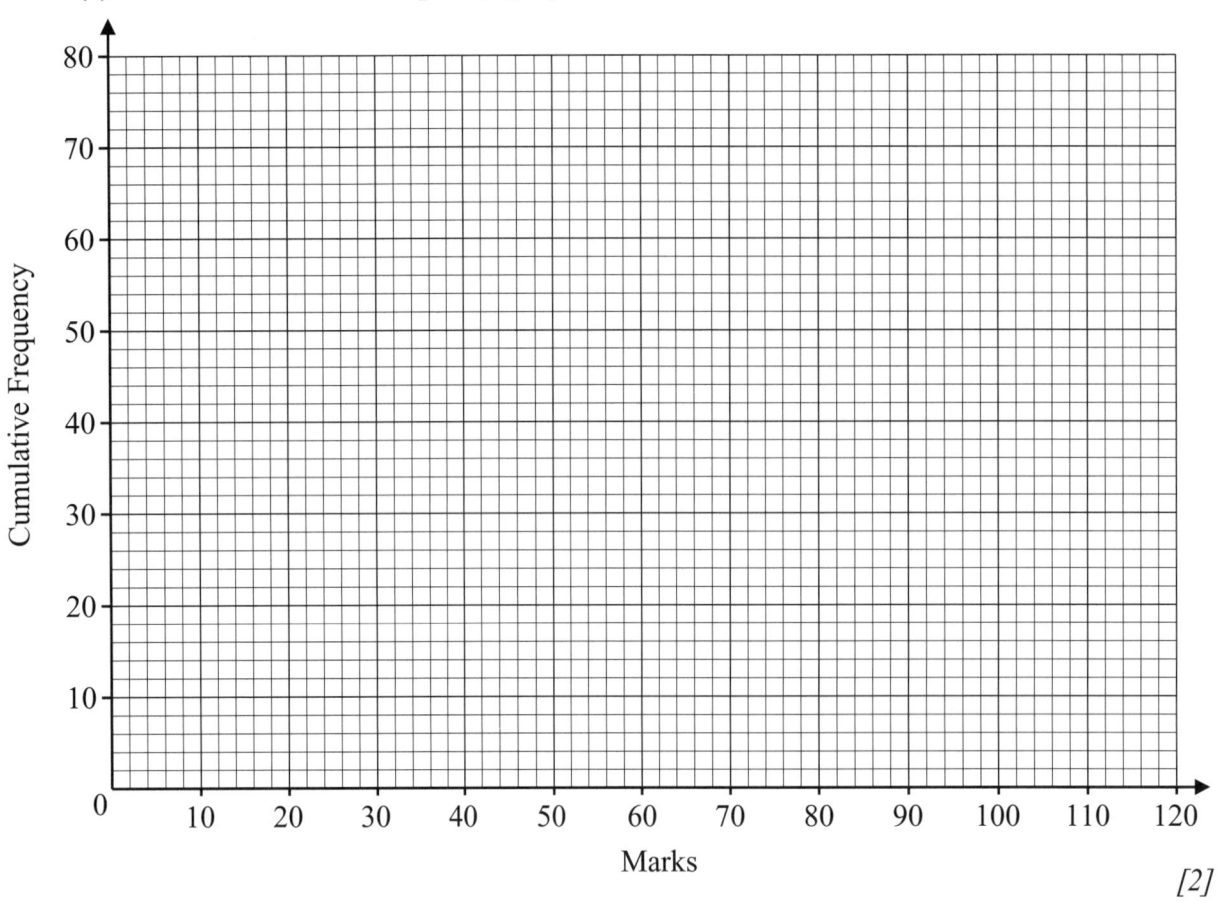

[2]

(b) Students with 90 or more marks are awarded either a platinum or a gold certificate.
Platinum and gold certificates are awarded in the ratio 1 : 1.5.
Students with the highest marks are awarded a platinum certificate.

Estimate the minimum mark needed to be awarded a platinum certificate.
Show how you get your answer.

[3]

[Total 5 marks]

8 Decide whether the triangle shown below is right-angled, making your reasoning clear.

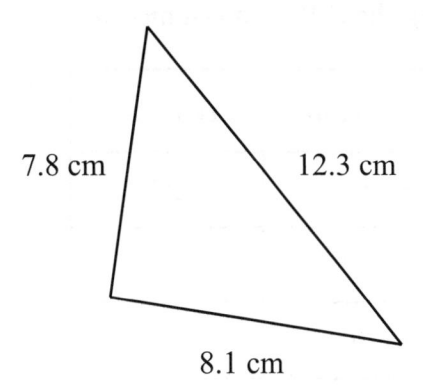

7.8 cm   12.3 cm
8.1 cm

[Total 3 marks]

9 Find the arc length of the sector shown below.
Give your answer in terms of π.

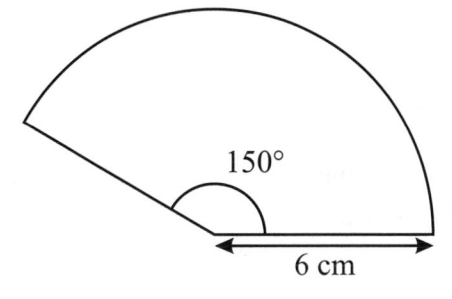

150°
6 cm

.... cm
[Total 2 marks]

7 Declan keeps chickens and weighs all the eggs they lay.
The table shows the weights of eggs he collected last month.

Mass (*m*) in grams	Frequency
$40 \leq m < 50$	27
$50 \leq m < 60$	30
$60 \leq m < 70$	16
$70 \leq m < 80$	7

(a) Calculate an estimate of the mean mass of Declan's eggs.

.... g
[3]

(b) Eggs are classified as small if they weigh 53 g or less.

Estimate the percentage of his eggs that would be classified as small.
Clearly describe any assumptions you make.

....

....

....

....

....

....

[3]

[Total 6 marks]

5 (a) Hamed and Javez are waiting together at a bus station.
Hamed's bus leaves every 18 minutes and Javez's bus leaves every 15 minutes.
The buses left the station at the same time at 2:00 pm.
When will the buses next leave the station at the same time?

....
[2]

(b) Explain an assumption you made in part (a).

....

....
[1]
[Total 3 marks]

6 Express $0.4\dot{1}$ as a fraction in its simplest form.

....
[Total 2 marks]

3 Alison, Boris and Che shared a lottery win in the ratio 7 : 3 : 2.

If Boris' share was £11 367, how much more did Alison get than Che?

£ ....
[Total 3 marks]

4 (a) Solve $2 - 4x \leq 12$

....
[2]

(b) n is an integer.
What is the smallest value of n that satisfies $2 - 4n \leq 12$?

$n = $ ....
[1]
[Total 3 marks]

Answer ALL the questions.

Write your answers in the spaces provided.

You must show all of your working.

1   The mass of a snowflake is 2.5 mg.
    1 000 000 mg = 1 kg.

    Convert the mass of the snowflake into kg.
    Give your answer in standard form.

    .... kg
    [Total 2 marks]

2   (a) Simplify $\dfrac{12x^4y^3}{2x^3y^7}$

    ....
    [2]

    (b) Solve $3(x-5) = 5x + 11$

    $x =$ ....
    [2]
    [Total 4 marks]

General Certificate of Secondary Education

GCSE
Mathematics (Grade 9-1)
Higher Tier

Practice Set 1
Paper 2: Calculator

Time allowed: 1 hour 30 minutes

Centre name

Centre number

Candidate number

Surname

Other names

Candidate signature

In addition to this paper you should have:
- A pen, pencil and eraser.
- A ruler.
- A protractor.
- A pair of compasses.
- A calculator.

Instructions to candidates

- Write your name and other details in the spaces provided above.
- Answer all questions in the spaces provided.
- In calculations show clearly how you worked out your answers.
- Diagrams are **not** drawn accurately unless otherwise indicated.
- Calculators may be used — if your calculator doesn't have a π button, take the value of π to be 3.142

Information for candidates

- There are 80 marks available for this paper.
- The marks available are given in brackets at the end of each question.
- You may get marks for method, even if your answer is incorrect.

Advice to candidates

- Work steadily through the paper.
- Don't spend too long on one question.
- If you have time at the end, go back and check your answers.

For examiner's use			
Q	Mark	Q	Mark
1		12	
2		13	
3		14	
4		15	
5		16	
6		17	
7		18	
8		19	
9		20	
10		21	
11			
Total			

22 The diagram shows a sketch of the circle with equation $x^2 + y^2 = 5$.
The y-coordinate of point A is -1.
The tangent to the circle at A crosses the axes at B and C as shown.

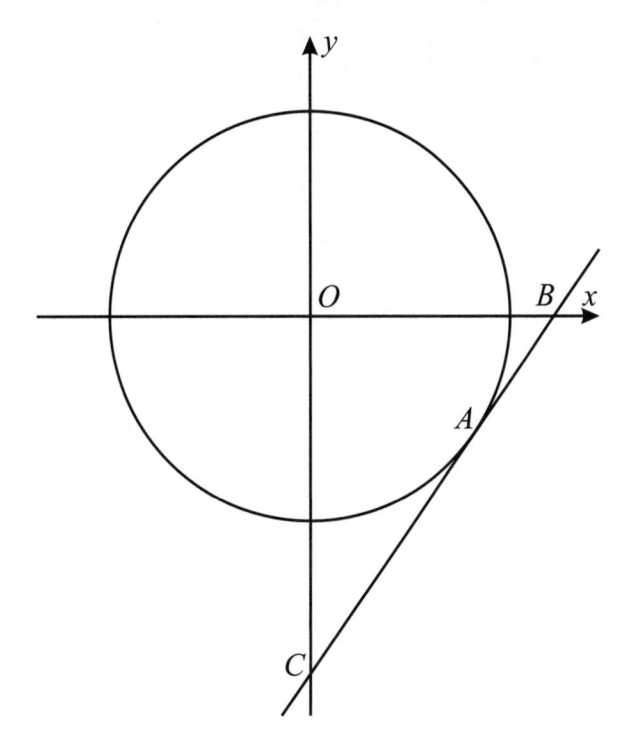

Find the area of triangle OBC.

....

[Total 5 marks]

[TOTAL FOR PAPER = 80 MARKS]

21 (a) Solve the simultaneous equations

$$x^2 + y^2 = 20$$
$$x - 3y = 10$$

x = ... y = ...

x = ... y = ...
[5]

(b) How many points of intersection are there for the graphs with equations $x^2 + y^2 = 20$ and $x - 3y = 10$? Explain your answer.

....

....

....
[1]

[Total 6 marks]

20 The triangular prism below has length l cm.

The ratio of the pressures exerted on the ground when the prism is stood on face A to when it is stood on face B is $3:5$.

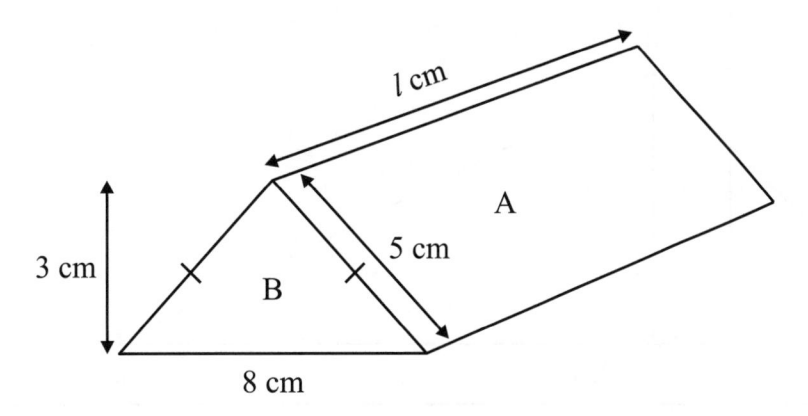

Find the missing length, l.

$l = $ .... cm

[Total 4 marks]

19 On a coordinate grid, $B = (-4, 1)$ and $C = (2, 1)$. Triangle ABC is isosceles.
Angle $ADC = 60°$.

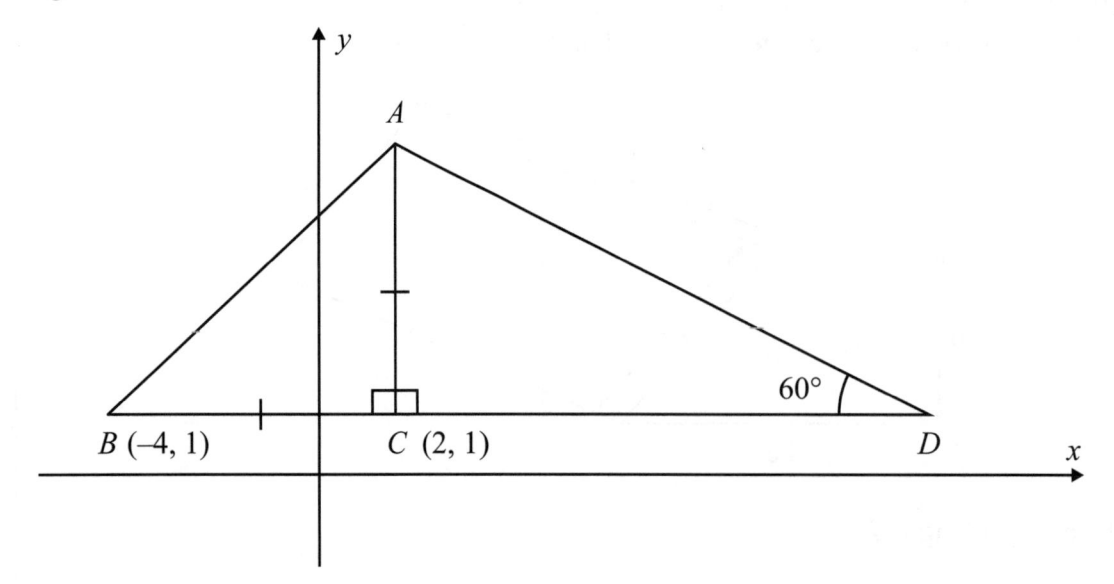

(a) Find an expression for the exact length of CD.
Give your answer in the form $a\sqrt{b}$, where a and b are integers.

$CD = $ ....
[4]

(b) Find an expression for the exact length of AD.
Give your answer in its simplest form.

$AD = $ ....
[2]

[Total 6 marks]

17 There is a sale on at a clothes shop.
All shorts are reduced by 10% and all jeans are reduced by 20%.

The ratio of the original price of jeans to the original price of shorts is 7:5.
The sale price of the shorts is £18.00.

What is the sale price of the jeans?

£ ....

[Total 4 marks]

18 Expand and simplify $(x+3)(x+5)(x-2)$

....

[Total 3 marks]

15 Find the value of:

(a) $\dfrac{10}{\sqrt{5}}$, giving your answer in the form $\sqrt{c}$, where c is an integer.

....
[3]

(b) $\left(1\dfrac{7}{9}\right)^{-1\frac{1}{2}}$, giving your answer in the form $\dfrac{a}{b}$, where a and b are integers.

....
[3]

[Total 6 marks]

16 The table shows a list of metals and their densities (in g/cm³).

Name of metal	Density (g/cm³)
Aluminium	2.7
Iron	8
Silver	10.5

A metal of volume 0.5 m³ has a mass of 4000 kg.
Which metal do you think this is? Show your working.

....
[Total 2 marks]

14 Nuala flew her drone at the beach for 10 minutes. The drone automatically recorded its horizontal velocity and Nuala was able to generate the following graph of the flight.

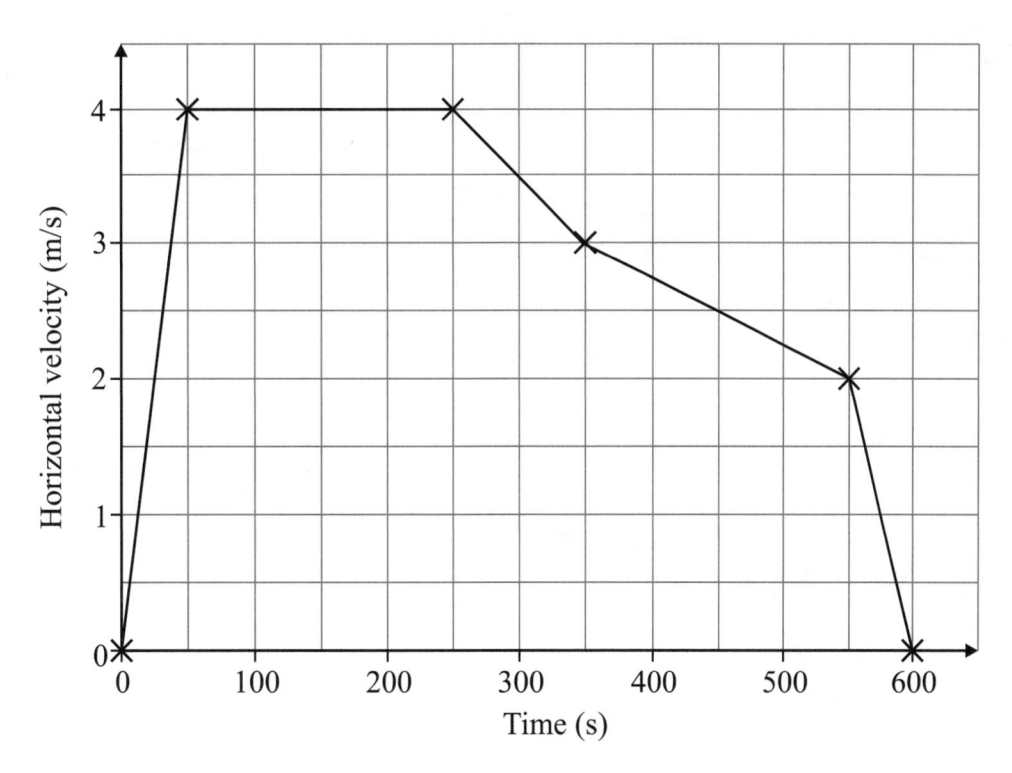

(a) Use the graph to work out the total horizontal distance covered by the drone.

.... m
[3]

(b) Write down the average horizontal acceleration of the drone.

.... m/s^2
[1]

[Total 4 marks]

13 ABC and DEF are parallel.
AG and BF are parallel.
AE = BE = EF
Angle DEG = 46°

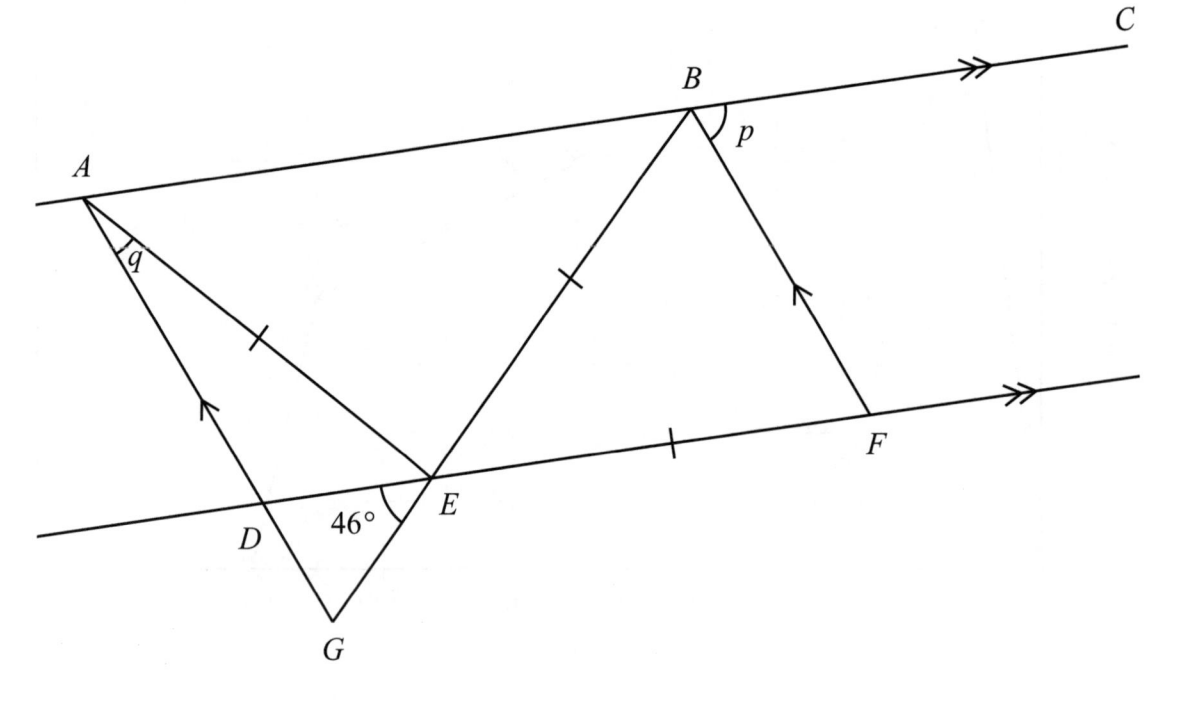

Find the size of the angles marked p and q.
You must show your working.

p = ... °

q = ... °

[Total 4 marks]

11 A child's set of building blocks contains 5 different colours.
One block is selected at random.
The table shows the probabilities of selecting a blue block and a green block.

Block Colour	Blue	Green	Orange	Red	Yellow
Probability	0.2	0.35			

The probability of picking out a green or orange block is 0.62
The probability of picking out a block that is not yellow is 0.92

Complete the table to show the probability of picking each block colour.

[Total 3 marks]

12 Two numbers are in the ratio 4 : 5.
Their highest common factor is 16.

(a) Find a possible pair of numbers.

.... and ....
[2]

(b) Are there any other possible pairs? Explain your answer.

....

....

....
[1]

[Total 3 marks]

10 Choose an equation from the box to match each of the graphs below.

| $y = \sin x$ | $y = \cos x$ | $y = x^2$ | $y = -x^2$ | $y = x^3$ | $y = -x^3$ |
| $y = -2^x$ | $y = 2^x$ | $y = \dfrac{1}{x}$ | $y = -\dfrac{1}{x}$ | | |

(a)

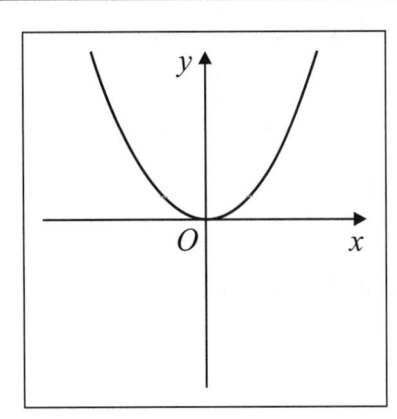

$y = $ ....
[1]

(b)

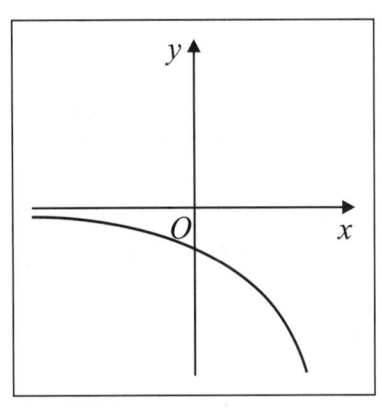

$y = $ ....
[1]

(c)

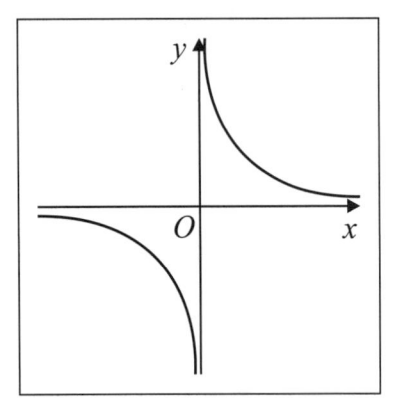

$y = $ ....
[1]

(d)

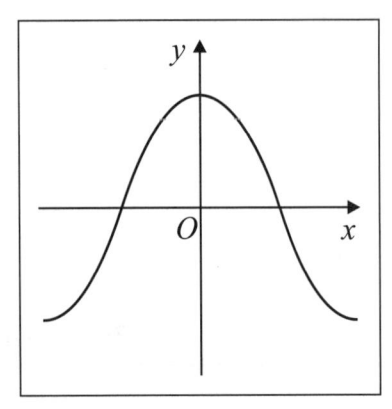

$y = $ ....
[1]

[Total 4 marks]

8 Alice has 2 dogs, Ollie and Taffy.
Ollie eats $\frac{2}{3}$ of a tin of dog food every day and Taffy eats $\frac{2}{5}$ of a tin every day.
Alice buys a crate of 24 tins.

How many whole days should the crate last?

.... days
[Total 3 marks]

9 Look at this calculation.
$$\frac{226 \times 0.074}{0.681}$$

(a) By rounding each number to 1 significant figure, work out an estimate to the calculation.

....
[2]

(b) Explain whether you think your answer to part (a) is an overestimate, underestimate or if it is impossible to tell.

....

....

....
[1]
[Total 3 marks]

7 Dom has been training for a half marathon.
He records the distances and times taken when he goes out running.

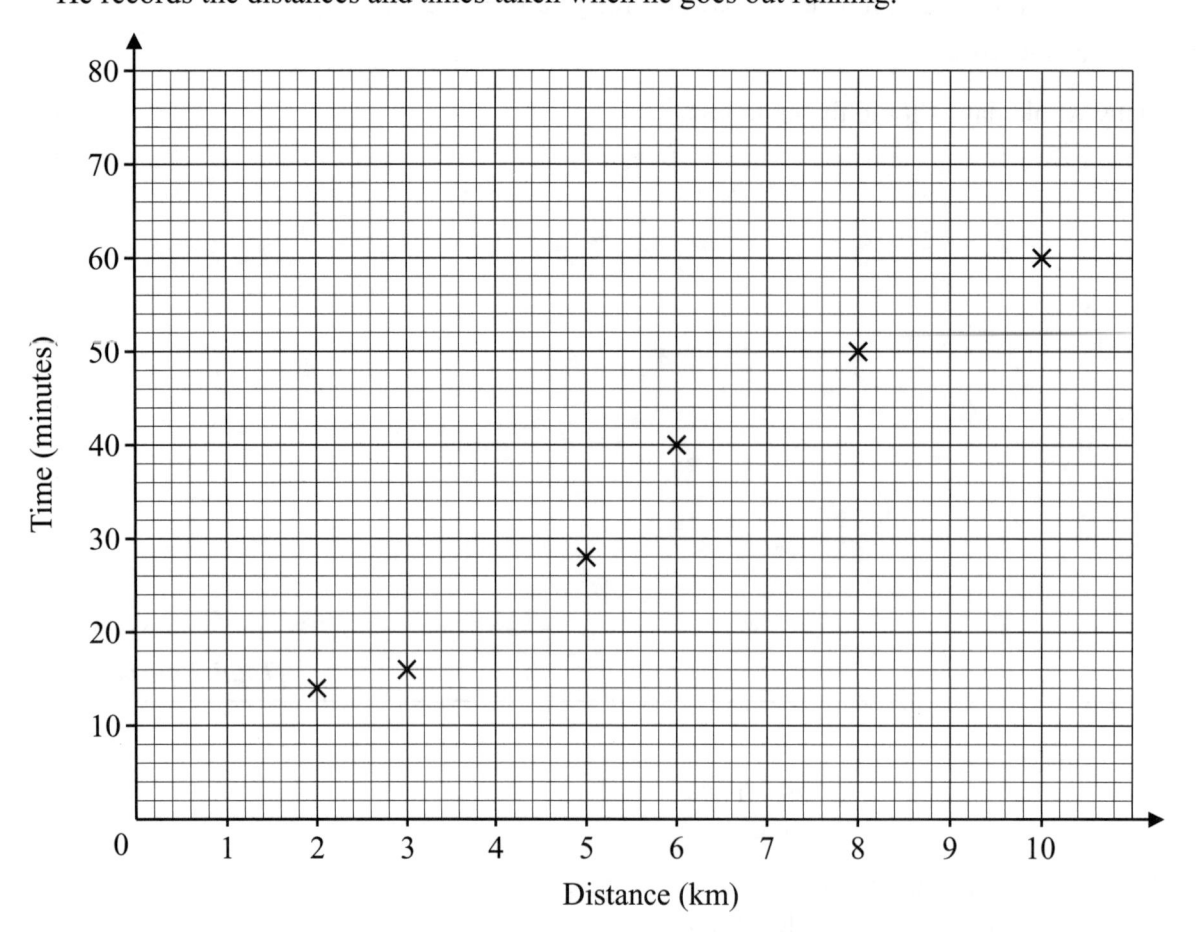

[Scatter graph with Distance (km) on x-axis from 0 to 10 and Time (minutes) on y-axis from 0 to 80, showing plotted points]

(a) Dom also completed a 4 km run in 21 minutes and a 9 km run in 62 minutes.
Plot these points on the graph.

[1]

(b) Use the graph to estimate how long it would take him to run 7.5 km.

.... minutes
[2]

(c) Why might you not expect the points to lie in a straight line?

....

....

....
[1]

[Total 4 marks]

5 The sets ξ, P and Q are shown below.

ξ = {positive integers less than or equal to 20}
P = {prime numbers}
Q = {1, 2, 3, 4, 6, 8, 12}

(a) List the members of the set P ∩ Q

....
[2]

(b) Find n(P ∪ Q)

....
[2]

[Total 4 marks]

6 Mathilde asks her group of friends whether they like Maths, PE or History lessons the most. She puts her results in a pie chart.

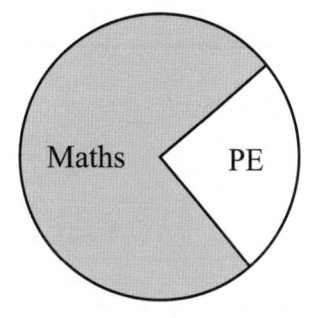

She claims that, "No one in my school likes History the most."
Do you agree with her statement? Explain your answer.

....

....

....

[Total 1 mark]

3 The diagram shows a prism.

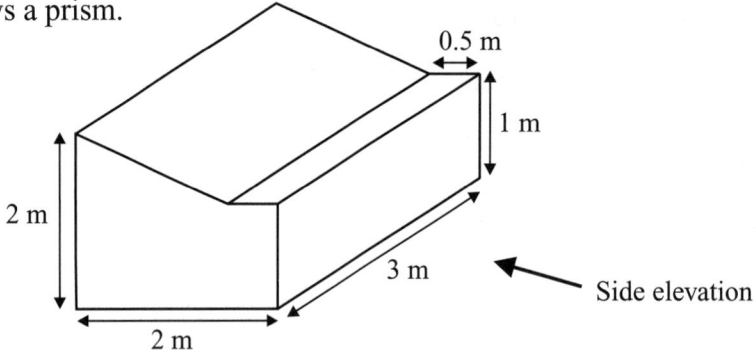

Using the scale shown on the grids, accurately draw the side elevation and plan view of the prism.

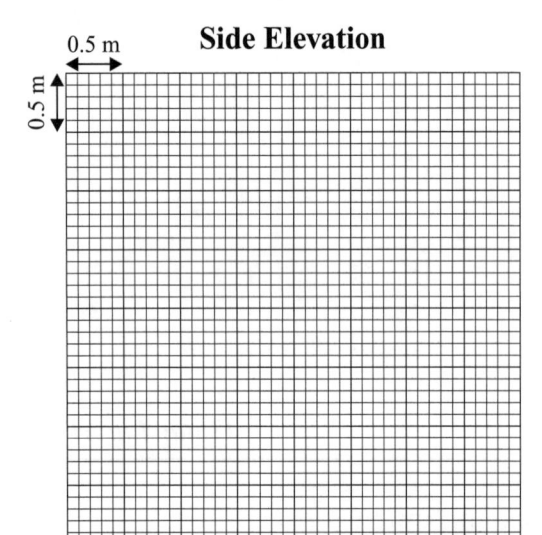

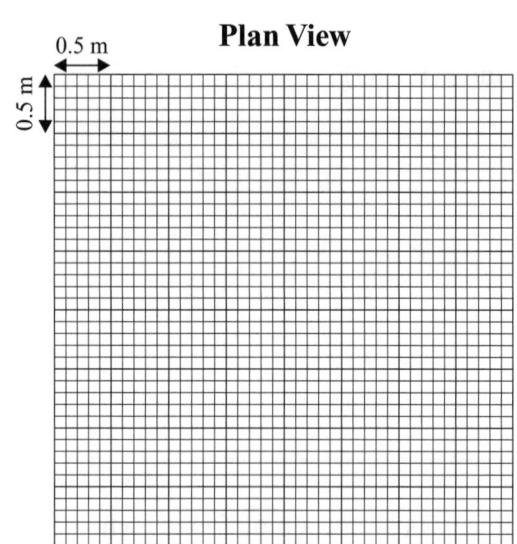

Side Elevation

Plan View

[Total 2 marks]

4 (a) Make y the subject of the formula $x = 3y - 5$

....
[2]

(b) Factorise the expression $8x^2 - 12xy$

....
[2]

[Total 4 marks]

Answer ALL the questions.

Write your answers in the spaces provided.

You must show all of your working.

1   **a** and **b** are column vectors such that $\mathbf{a} = \begin{pmatrix} 8 \\ 3 \end{pmatrix}$ and $\mathbf{b} = \begin{pmatrix} 1 \\ -7 \end{pmatrix}$. Calculate:

(a) 3**a**

....
[1]

(b) **a** – 4**b**

....
[2]

[Total 3 marks]

2   140% of x is 28.
Find the value of x.

$x = $ ....

[Total 2 marks]

General Certificate of Secondary Education

GCSE
Mathematics (Grade 9-1)
Higher Tier

Practice Set 1
Paper 1: Non-calculator

Time allowed: 1 hour 30 minutes

Centre name				
Centre number				
Candidate number				

Surname	
Other names	
Candidate signature	

In addition to this paper you should have:
- A pen, pencil and eraser.
- A ruler.
- A protractor.
- A pair of compasses.

Calculators may **not** be used.

Instructions to candidates
- Write your name and other details in the spaces provided above.
- Answer all questions in the spaces provided.
- In calculations show clearly how you worked out your answers.
- Diagrams are **not** drawn accurately unless otherwise indicated.

Information for candidates
- There are 80 marks available for this paper.
- The marks available are given in brackets at the end of each question.
- You may get marks for method, even if your answer is incorrect.

Advice to candidates
- Work steadily through the paper.
- Don't spend too long on one question.
- If you have time at the end, go back and check your answers.

For examiner's use

Q	Mark	Q	Mark
1		12	
2		13	
3		14	
4		15	
5		16	
6		17	
7		18	
8		19	
9		20	
10		21	
11		22	
Total			

Exam Set MHB45 / MXHP43

20 A bag contains red beads and blue beads.
The probability of picking out a red bead is r.
One bead is picked out from the bag, its colour noted, and then it is replaced.
A second bead is then picked out.

The probability that exactly one of the beads is red is $\frac{4}{9}$.

(a) Find the possible values of r. Give your answer as a fraction in its simplest form.

$2r(1-r) = \frac{4}{9}$

$9r(1-r) = 2$

$9r^2 - 9r + 2 = 0$

$(3r - 1)(3r - 2) = 0$

$r = \dfrac{1}{3}$ and $r = \dfrac{2}{3}$

[4]

(b) Isaac counts the number of beads in the bag and says,
"The number of blue beads and the number of red beads are both odd."

Do you think Isaac is correct? Explain your answer.

No. If $r = \frac{1}{3}$, then the ratio of red to blue beads is 1 : 2, so the number of blue beads must be even. If $r = \frac{2}{3}$, the ratio is 2 : 1, so the number of red beads must be even. In either case, they cannot both be odd.

[2]

[Total 6 marks]

[TOTAL FOR PAPER = 80 MARKS]

19 *OABCD* is a square based pyramid.
The vertex *O* is vertically above the centre of the horizontal base *ABCD*.
OA = 12 cm and *AD* = 8 cm

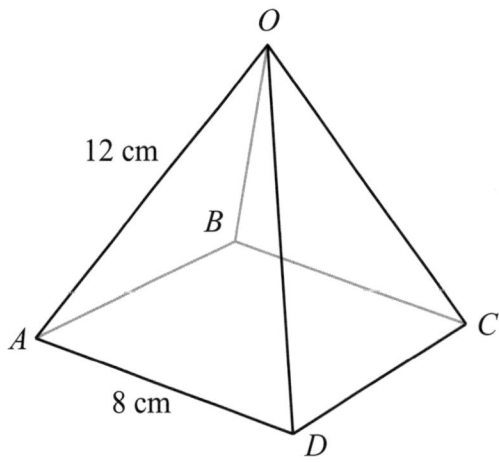

(a) Find the vertical height of the pyramid.
Find your answer in the form $a\sqrt{b}$, where *a* and *b* are integers.

.... cm
[3]

(b) Find the angle *OA* makes with the base *ABCD*.
Give your answer to 3 significant figures.

.... °
[3]

[Total 6 marks]

18 (a) Show that the equation $x^3 + 4x^2 - 13 = 0$ has a solution between the values $x = 1$ and $x = 2$.

[2]

(b) Show that the equation above can be rearranged to give $x = \sqrt{\dfrac{13 - x^3}{4}}$

[2]

(c) Use the iteration formula $x_{n+1} = \sqrt{\dfrac{13 - x_n^3}{4}}$, with $x_0 = 1.5$, to find an estimate for a solution of $x^3 + 4x^2 - 13 = 0$ to 2 decimal places.

$x = $ ....

[3]

[Total 7 marks]

17 Solve the following inequality.

(a) $x^2 - 1 \leq 3(x + 3)$

....
[4]

(b) Show your answer to part (a) on a number line in the space below.

[1]
[Total 5 marks]

16 The frequency table and histogram show the times taken by entrants to complete a fun run.

Time (*m*) in minutes	Frequency
$10 \leq m < 12$	8
$12 \leq m < 15$	
$15 \leq m < 20$	30
$20 \leq m < 25$	
$25 \leq m < 40$	30

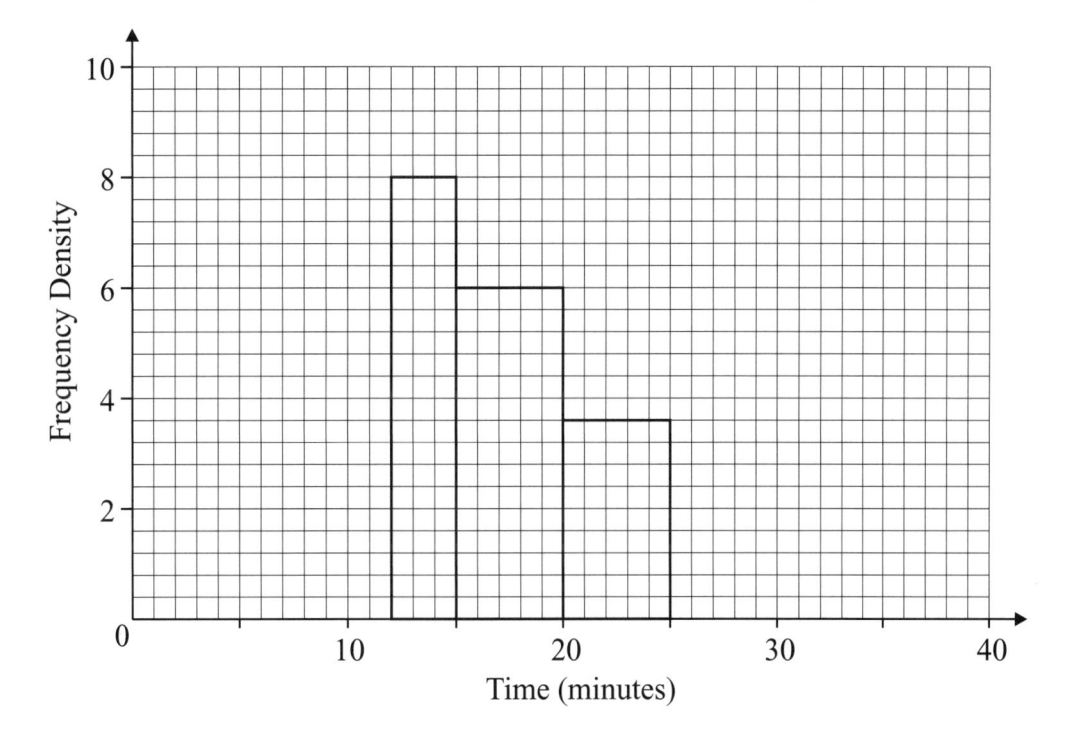

(a) Complete the histogram and frequency table.

[4]

(b) Harry competed in the fun run.
He boasts to his friends that the fun run was 10 km long.

Do you think Harry is telling the truth?
Give a reason for your answer.

....

....

....

....

[2]

[Total 6 marks]

15 Joel has been asked to paint the wooden table tops and sides on the outdoor tables at the café he works at. There are 20 tables to be painted.

Each table has a cylindrical top with a diameter of 90 cm and is 3 cm thick.

He has a 2.5 litre tin of paint with the following guidelines.

Covers 12 m² per litre
Allow 2 coats

(a) Can he paint all of the tables using his tin of paint?
You must show your working.

....
[5]

(b) Describe any assumptions that you made when calculating your answer to part (a).

....

....

....
[1]
[Total 6 marks]

14 Kelvin drops a rubber ball from a height of 140 cm onto concrete.
After each bounce, the ball rises to a height 24% less than the height it fell from.

(a) What height would the ball bounce to after it has hit the ground for the 5th time?
Give your answer to 1 decimal place.

.... cm
[3]

(b) How many times will the ball have bounced when
it fails to reach a height of 10 cm for the first time?

....
[2]
[Total 5 marks]

13 The table shows the population and area of four countries.

Country	Population	Area (km²)
Afghanistan	3.26×10^7	6.52×10^5
Austria	8.67×10^6	8.39×10^4
Morocco	3.33×10^7	4.47×10^5
Malaysia	3.05×10^7	3.30×10^5

(a) Which two countries are closest in terms of their population?
You must show your working.

....

....

....

....
[2]

(b) Population density is measured as the number of people per square kilometre.
Which country has the greatest population density?

....
[2]

[Total 4 marks]

11 A metal cone has a height of 4.3 cm and the radius of its base is 1.2 cm.
The mass of the cone is 17.5 g.

Work out the density of the cone in g/cm³.
Give your answer to a suitable degree of accuracy.

$$\text{Volume of a cone} = \frac{\pi r^2 h}{3}$$

.... g/cm³

[Total 3 marks]

12 A regular polygon has n sides and interior angles of 160°.

Find the size of each interior angle in a regular polygon with $4n$ sides.

.... °

[Total 3 marks]

9 The mean of the numbers x, 7, 13 and y is 8.
The range of the numbers is 16.
x is a negative integer.

Find the values of x and y.

$x =$ ....

$y =$ ....

[Total 4 marks]

10 John completes a 400 m wheelchair race in 64.5 seconds.
The distance is correct to the nearest metre and the time to the nearest half second.

Work out the lower bound of his average speed.

.... m/s

[Total 3 marks]

7 The diagram shows the triangle *PQR* with sides of length $5x - 18$, $3x - 5$ and $x + 6$.

Is triangle *PQR* equilateral?
You must show your working.

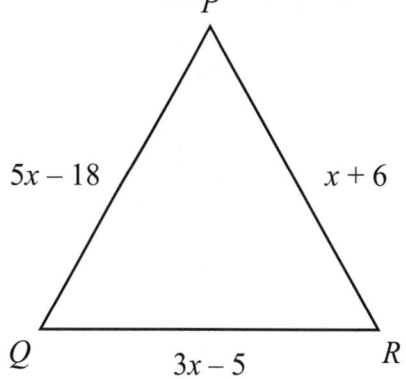

[Total 4 marks]

8 Chris is decorating cupcakes for a party. He has 5 different colours of icing, $n + 1$ different fondant animals and $n - 1$ types of sprinkles.

Each cupcake will have icing, a fondant animal and sprinkles on it.

There are 120 different ways to decorate the cupcakes.
What is the value of *n*?

$n = $ ....

[Total 2 marks]

6 (a) Draw the graph with equation $y = 3x - 4$ for values of x between -1 and 4.

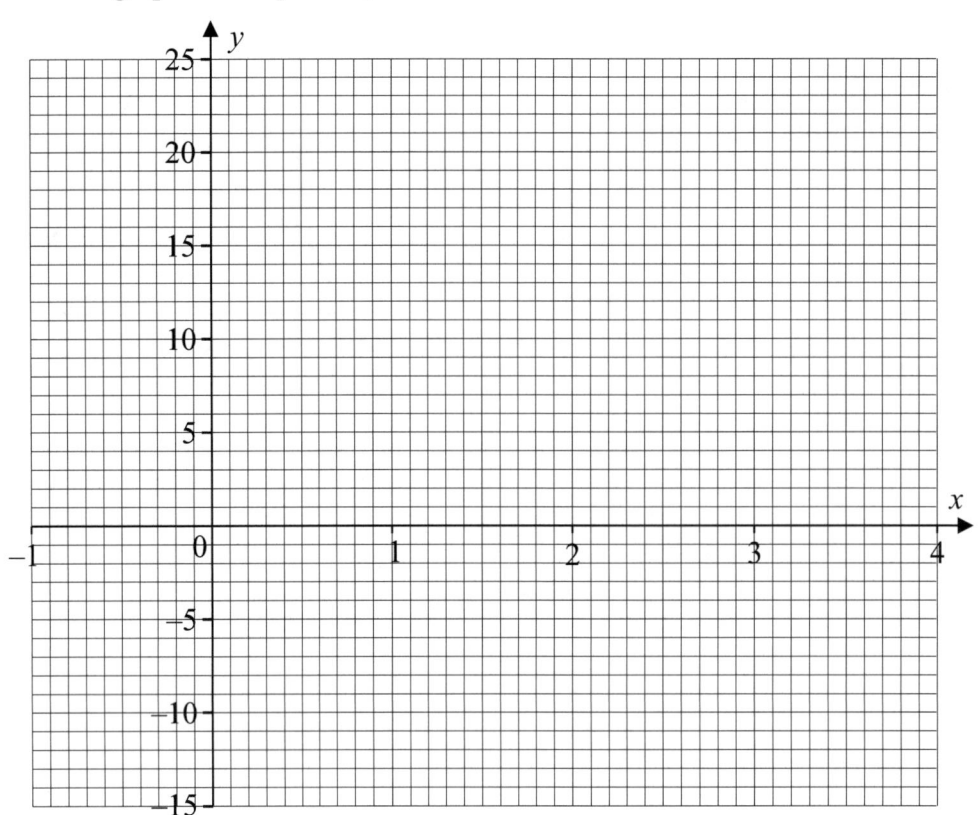

[2]

(b) Write down the equation of the graph parallel to $y = 3x - 4$ that passes through the point $(-1, 0)$.

....

[2]

[Total 4 marks]

4 Anton is on holiday in Mexico.
The exchange rate is £5 = 126 pesos

He finds a camera that he bought in the UK for £79.99 on sale for 1800 pesos.

Explain where the camera is cheaper and by how much.
Give your answer in pounds.

....

....

....

....

....

....

[Total 3 marks]

5 The first three patterns of a sequence are shown below.

How many white dots will be in the 1000th pattern?

....

[Total 2 marks]

3 A, B and C are points on a coordinate grid. CAB is a straight line.

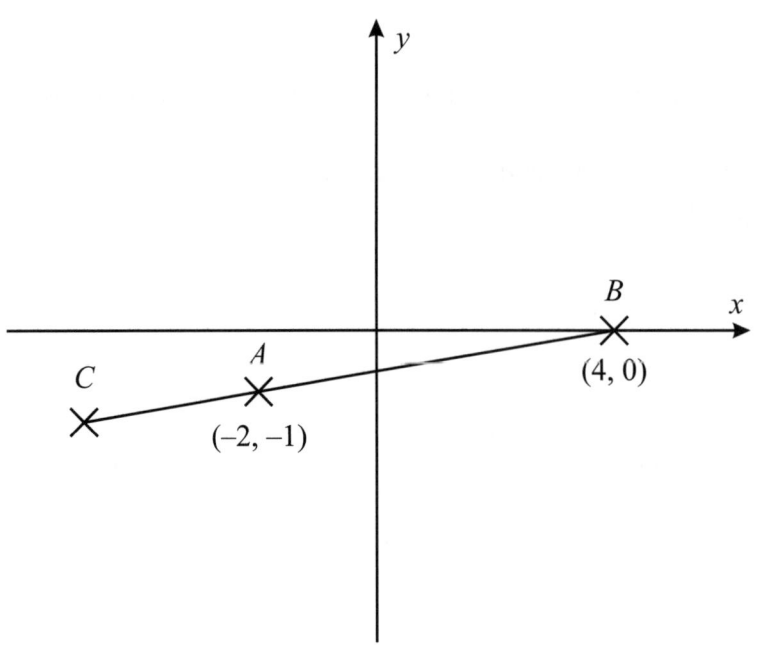

(a) Write down the column vector that translates point A onto point B.

....
[1]

(b) AB is twice the length of AC.
Use your answer to part (a) to write down the column vector that translates point A onto point C.

....
[1]
[Total 2 marks]

Answer ALL the questions.

Write your answers in the spaces provided.

You must show all of your working.

1   The number n expressed as a product of prime factors is $2^3 \times 3^2 \times 5$.

Write n^2 as a product of prime factors.

$n^2 = $ ....

[Total 1 mark]

2   Lola has a recipe for lentil soup that she plans to make for 25 people at a party.

Lentil Soup *(4 servings)*
100 g lentils   2 sticks of celery
240 g carrots   1 litre vegetable stock
180 g sweet potato

(a) She only has 500 g of sweet potato.
How much more sweet potato does she need to buy?

.... g
[3]

(b) How many grams of lentils would she need to make a soup for n people?

.... g
[1]

[Total 4 marks]

General Certificate of Secondary Education

GCSE
Mathematics (Grade 9-1)
Higher Tier

Practice Set 1
Paper 3: Calculator

Time allowed: 1 hour 30 minutes

| Centre name |
| Centre number |
| Candidate number |

| Surname |
| Other names |
| Candidate signature |

In addition to this paper you should have:
- A pen, pencil and eraser.
- A ruler.
- A protractor.
- A pair of compasses.
- A calculator.

Instructions to candidates
- Write your name and other details in the spaces provided above.
- Answer all questions in the spaces provided.
- In calculations show clearly how you worked out your answers.
- Diagrams are **not** drawn accurately unless otherwise indicated.
- Calculators may be used — if your calculator doesn't have a π button, take the value of π to be 3.142

Information for candidates
- There are 80 marks available for this paper.
- The marks available are given in brackets at the end of each question.
- You may get marks for method, even if your answer is incorrect.

Advice to candidates
- Work steadily through the paper.
- Don't spend too long on one question.
- If you have time at the end, go back and check your answers.

For examiner's use

Q	Mark	Q	Mark
1		11	
2		12	
3		13	
4		14	
5		15	
6		16	
7		17	
8		18	
9		19	
10		20	
Total			

19 A rectangular field, *ABCD*, has lengths such that:

$AB = CD$, $BC = AD$ and $AB > BC$

$AB = \dfrac{1}{3x}$ miles, $BC = \dfrac{x}{6}$ miles.

The perimeter of the field is exactly 1 mile.

Find the lengths of sides *AB* and *BC*.

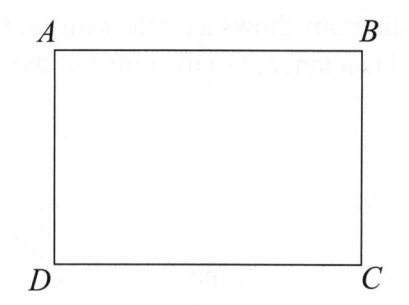

Perimeter: $2\left(\dfrac{1}{3x} + \dfrac{x}{6}\right) = 1$

$\dfrac{1}{3x} + \dfrac{x}{6} = \dfrac{1}{2}$

Multiply by $6x$: $2 + x^2 = 3x$

$x^2 - 3x + 2 = 0$

$(x-1)(x-2) = 0$, so $x = 1$ or $x = 2$.

Since $AB > BC$: $\dfrac{1}{3x} > \dfrac{x}{6}$ gives $x^2 < 2$, so $x = 1$.

AB = ... $\dfrac{1}{3}$ miles

BC = ... $\dfrac{1}{6}$ miles

[Total 5 marks]

[TOTAL FOR PAPER = 80 MARKS]

18 The diagram shows a circle with centre (0, 0).
Line *l* is a tangent to the circle at the point $P(-8, -6)$.

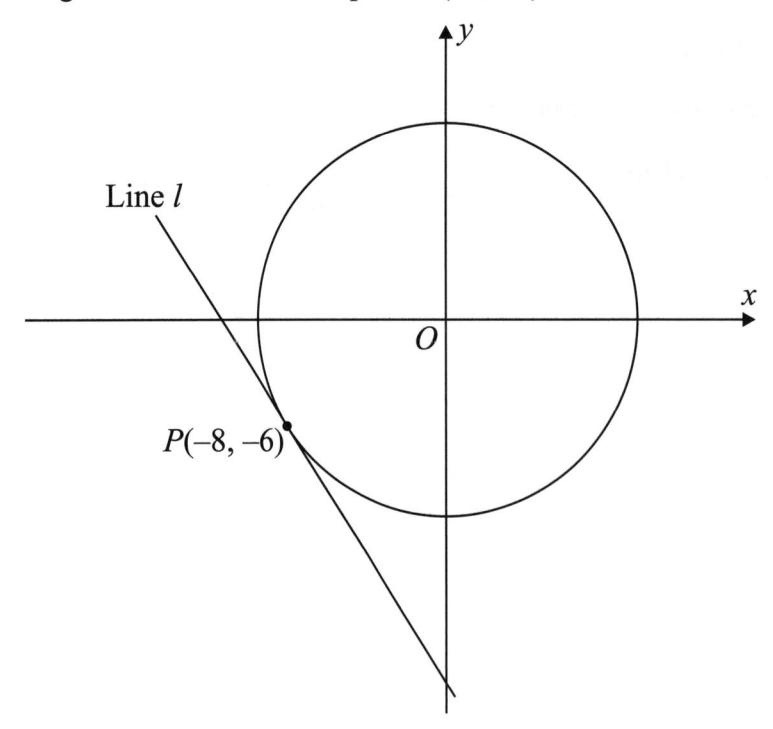

Find the equation of line *l*.

....
[Total 4 marks]

17 A frustum is made by removing a small cone from the pointed end of a full cone. The small cone and the frustum have the same height.
Find the following ratio in its simplest form.

Volume of the small cone : Volume of frustum

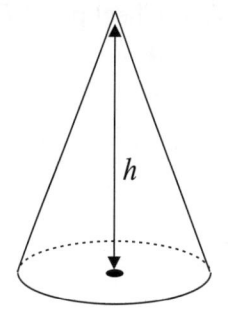

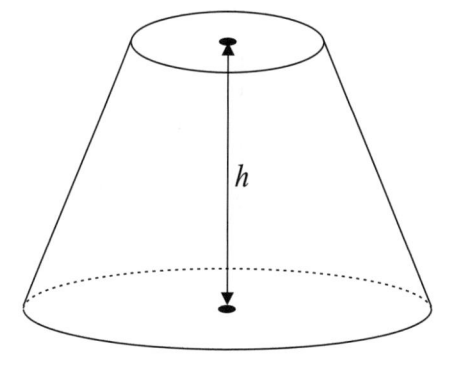

Volume of cone = $\frac{1}{3}\pi r^2 h$

....

[Total 4 marks]

16 During an orienteering competition, Mhairi runs 457 m on a bearing of 060° from Checkpoint *C* to Checkpoint *D*. She then runs 350 m on a bearing of 160° to Checkpoint *E*.

Calculate the direct distance from Checkpoint *E* to Checkpoint *C*.
Give your answer to 1 decimal place.

.... m

[Total 4 marks]

14 A, B, C and D are points on the circumference of a circle.
Angle BAD = x + 18°
Angle BCD = 5x + 12°
Angle ADC = 43°

Show that ABCD is a trapezium.

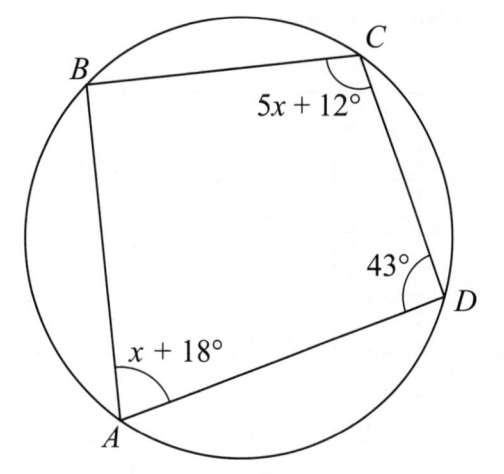

[Total 4 marks]

15 A sequence is defined by the term-to-term rule $u_{n+1} = (u_n)^2 - 3u_n - 1$

(a) If $u_1 = 5$, show that $u_3 = 53$

[2]

(b) If $u_1 = 3$, what is the value of u_{171}?

u_{171} = ...
[3]

[Total 5 marks]

13 The time taken for students to travel to school was recorded.
The histogram shows the results.

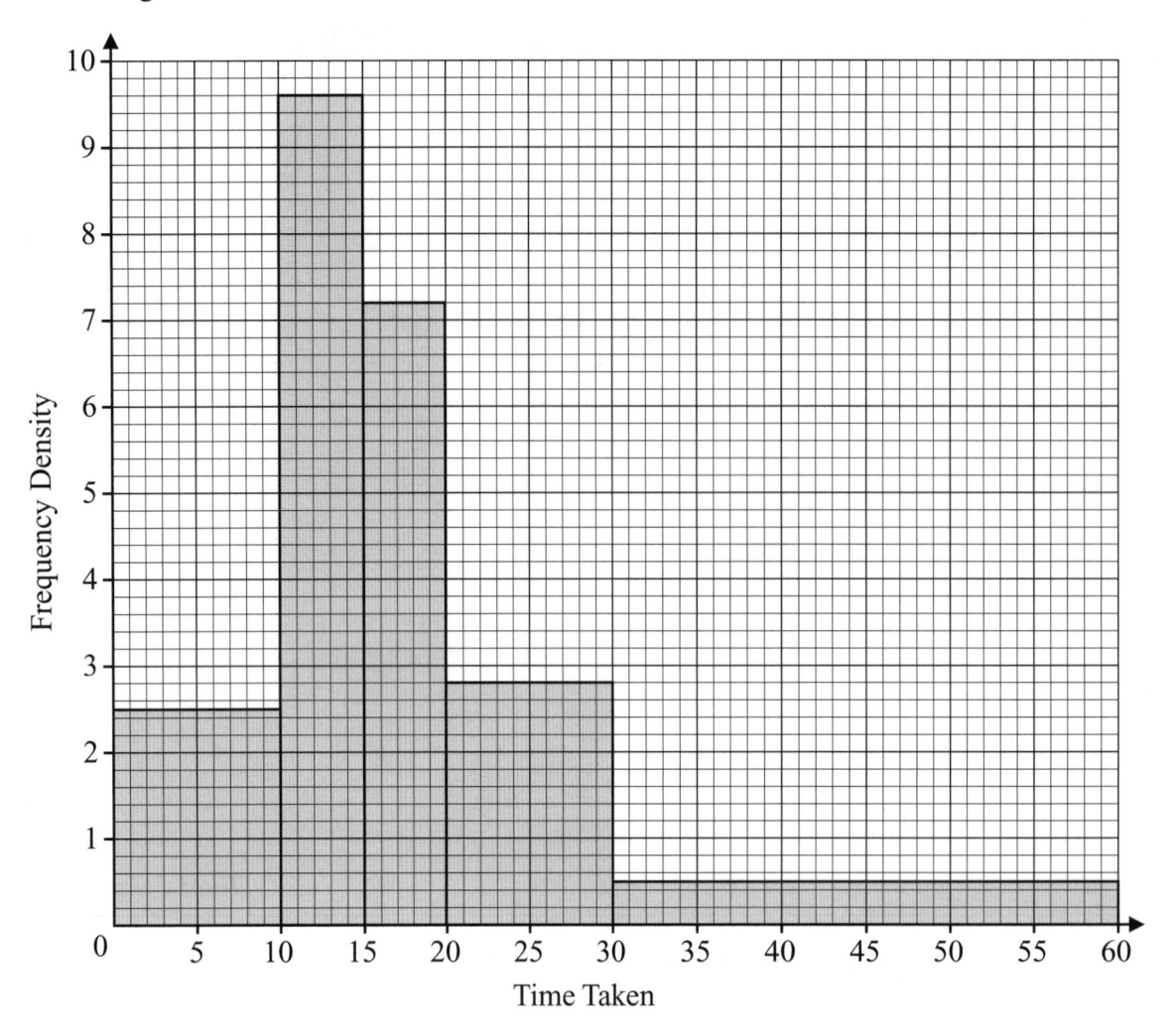

(a) Use the histogram to complete the grouped frequency table below.

Time taken (t)	$0 < t \leq 10$	$10 < t \leq 15$	$15 < t \leq 20$	$20 < t \leq 30$	$30 < t \leq 60$
Frequency					

[2]

(b) The school day begins at 8:40 am. Estimate the number of students who must leave home before 8:15 am if they are to arrive at school on time.

....
[3]

[Total 5 marks]

12 Antony is drawing a scale diagram of a show garden.
On the diagram the scale is 1 cm = 1 m.
Lines *AB*, *BC*, *CD* and *AD* make up the boundaries of the garden.

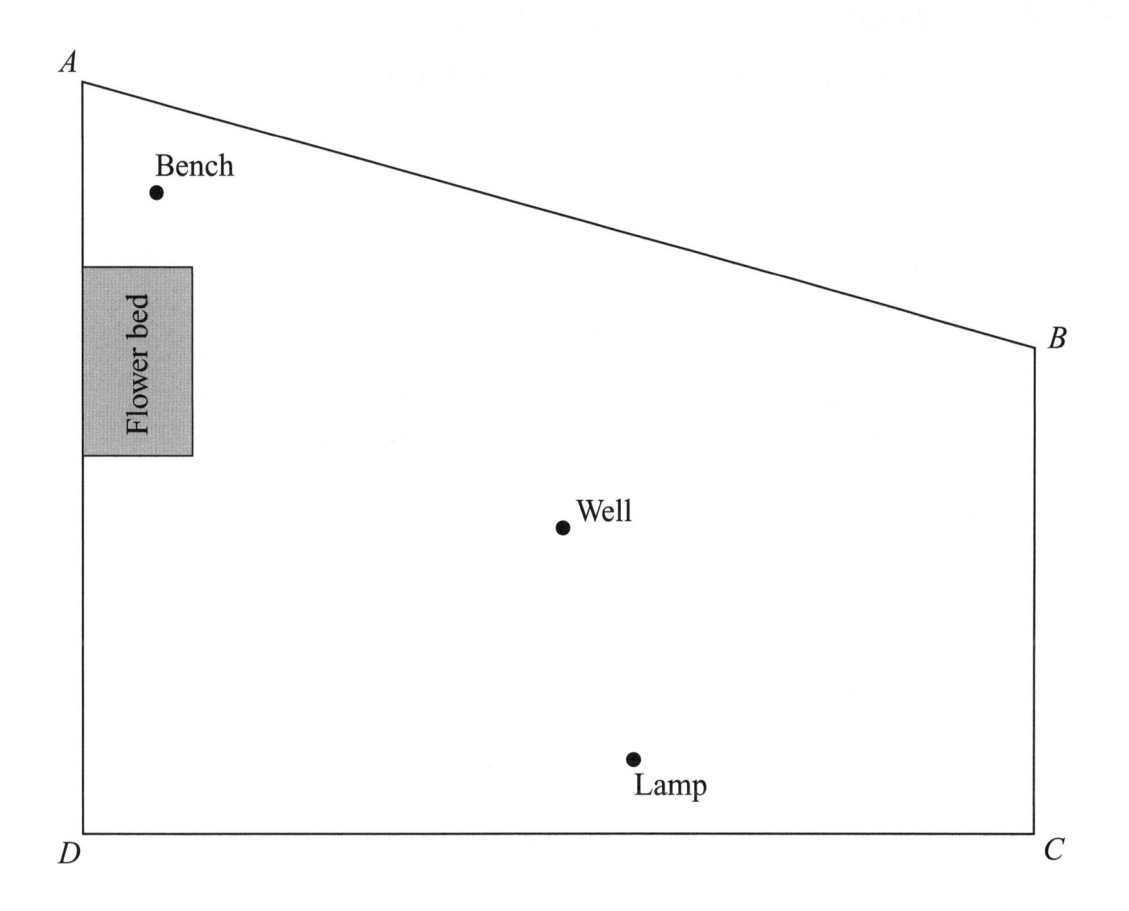

(a) A fountain is placed closer to the bench than the well, and within 3 m of boundary *CD*.

Shade the area in which the fountain is placed.
Show all of your construction lines.

[3]

(b) An electrical wire runs from a point on boundary *AB* to the lamp.

What is the shortest length that the wire could be?
Show all of your construction lines.

.... m
[2]

[Total 5 marks]

11 In a basketball game, Jack takes two shots.

The probability that Jack scores with the first shot is 0.7
The probability of Jack scoring with both shots is 0.56
The probability of Jack missing with both shots is 0.18

(a) Complete the tree diagram to show these probabilities:

First shot   **Second shot**

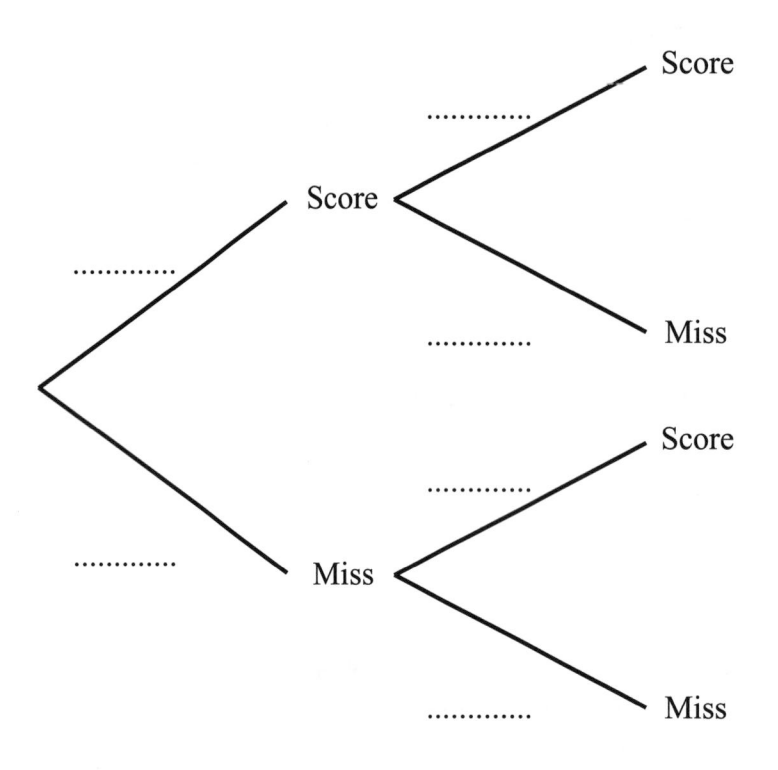

```
              ............. Score
      Score <
  .....     ............. Miss
 <
  .....     ............. Score
      Miss <
              ............. Miss
```

[3]

(b) Given that Jack scores with exactly one shot, is it more likely that Jack missed his first or his second shot? Show your working.

....

[3]

[Total 6 marks]

9 $\mathbf{a} = \begin{pmatrix} 2 \\ -1 \end{pmatrix}$ $\mathbf{b} = \begin{pmatrix} 5 \\ 3 \end{pmatrix}$

If $m\mathbf{a} + n\mathbf{b} = \begin{pmatrix} 1 \\ -6 \end{pmatrix}$, find the values of m and n.

$m = $ ....

$n = $ ....

[Total 4 marks]

10 Eddie drove from Carlisle to Preston in 1 hour 45 minutes, at an average speed of 60 mph. He then drove a further 23 miles to Blackpool in 35 minutes.

Find Eddie's average speed for his journey from Carlisle to Blackpool, to the nearest 1 mph.

.... mph

[Total 3 marks]

8 A scientist models the population of a colony of penguins using the formula $P = 8000 \times 0.93^t$, where t is the number of years after 2015.

(a) Write down the value of P in 2015.

$P =$ ....
[1]

(b) Find the number of penguins that the model predicts there will be in 2018.

....
[2]

(c) How many whole years after 2015 is the population of penguins predicted to have fallen below 5000?

....
[2]

[Total 5 marks]

7 The diagram shows part of a 16-sided regular polygon.

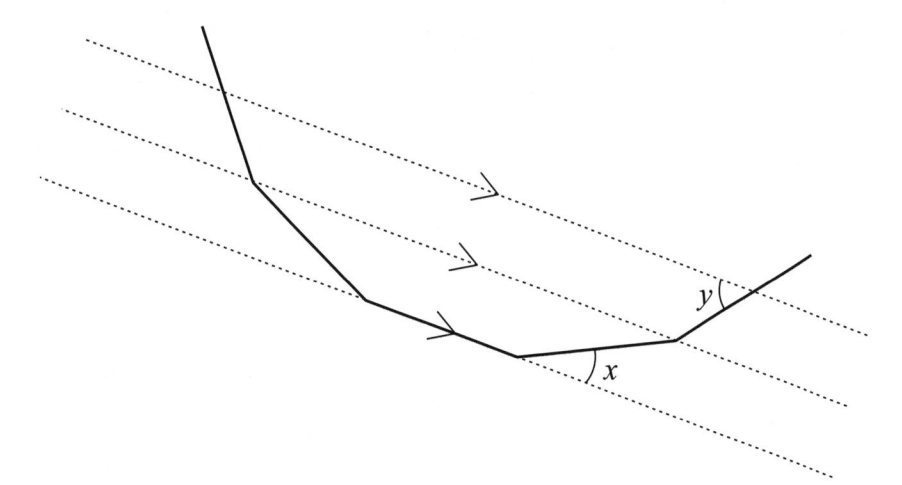

(a) Calculate the size of angle *x*.

x = ...°
[1]

(b) Calculate the size of angle *y*.

y = ...°
[2]

[Total 3 marks]

5 Show clearly that $16^{-\frac{3}{2}} = \frac{1}{64}$

[Total 2 marks]

6 (a) Solve $2x - 5 < 5x + 4$

....
[2]

(b) Show the solution on this number line.

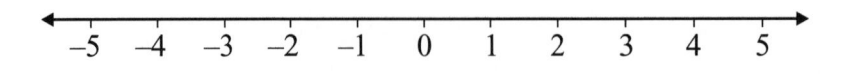

[1]

[Total 3 marks]

4 Two stationery shops have special offers on sticky notes.

Shop A: £2.65 for 160 sticky notes + 25% extra free

Shop B: £2.98 for 160 sticky notes — buy 1, get 1 half price

Harold needs to buy 2700 sticky notes for his business.
Which shop would be cheaper? Show your working.

....

[Total 4 marks]

2   A DVD that costs £8.99 on a British internet shopping website costs $12.99 on an American website and €10.99 on a French website.

Exchange rates for dollars, pounds and euros are shown below:

£1 = $1.43   €1 = £0.81

Which website is selling the DVD for the cheapest price?

....
[Total 3 marks]

3   The width of a rectangular room is 5.4 m, truncated to 1 decimal place.

(a) Find the error interval for the width, w.

....
[2]

The length of the room is 12.3 m, correct to 3 significant figures.

(b) Find the smallest possible area of the room.

.... m^2
[3]
[Total 5 marks]

1 (a) Simplify $3x + 5y + 7y - 9x - y$

....
[1]

(b) Factorise $20x^3y + 8xy^2$

....
[2]

(c) Solve $\dfrac{3x + 4}{2} = \dfrac{5x + 3}{3}$

$x = $ ....
[3]

[Total 6 marks]

General Certificate of Secondary Education

GCSE Mathematics (Grade 9-1) Higher Tier

Practice Set 2
Paper 3: Calculator

Time allowed: 1 hour 30 minutes

Centre name	
Centre number	
Candidate number	

Surname	
Other names	
Candidate signature	

In addition to this paper you should have:
- A pen, pencil and eraser.
- A ruler.
- A protractor.
- A pair of compasses.
- A calculator.

Instructions to candidates
- Write your name and other details in the spaces provided above.
- Answer all questions in the spaces provided.
- In calculations show clearly how you worked out your answers.
- Diagrams are **not** drawn accurately unless otherwise indicated.
- Calculators may be used — if your calculator doesn't have a π button, take the value of π to be 3.142

Information for candidates
- There are 80 marks available for this paper.
- The marks available are given in brackets at the end of each question.
- You may get marks for method, even if your answer is incorrect.

Advice to candidates
- Work steadily through the paper.
- Don't spend too long on one question.
- If you have time at the end, go back and check your answers.

For examiner's use

Q	Mark	Q	Mark
1		11	
2		12	
3		13	
4		14	
5		15	
6		16	
7		17	
8		18	
9		19	
10			
Total			

Exam Set MHB45 / MXHP43